GUIDELINES FOR WRITING AND PREPARING A MANUSCRIPT FOR INTERNATIONAL PUBLICATION

LANGUAGES AND LINGUISTICS

Additional books in this series can be found on Nova's website under the Series tab.

Additional E-books in this series can be found on Nova's website under the E-books tab.

PROFESSIONS – TRAINING, EDUCATION AND DEMOGRAPHICS

Additional books in this series can be found on Nova's website under the Series tab.

Additional E-books in this series can be found on Nova's website under the E-books tab.

LANGUAGES AND LINGUISTICS

GUIDELINES FOR WRITING AND PREPARING A MANUSCRIPT FOR INTERNATIONAL PUBLICATION

ABDEL-FATTAH Z. M. SALEM
J. L. TINOCO-JARAMILLO
D. CARDOSO-JIMÉNEZ
L.M.CAMACHO-DÍAZ
M. CIPRIANO-SALAZAR
AND
J. F. VÁZQUEZ-ARMIJO

Nova Science Publishers, Inc.
New York

NOTICE TO THE READER

The Publisher has taken reasonable care in the preparation of this book, but makes no expressed or implied warranty of any kind and assumes no responsibility for any errors or omissions. No liability is assumed for incidental or consequential damages in connection with or arising out of information contained in this book. The Publisher shall not be liable for any special, consequential, or exemplary damages resulting, in whole or in part, from the readers' use of, or reliance upon, this material.

Independent verification should be sought for any data, advice or recommendations contained in this book. In addition, no responsibility is assumed by the publisher for any injury and/or damage to persons or property arising from any methods, products, instructions, ideas or otherwise contained in this publication.

This publication is designed to provide accurate and authoritative information with regard to the subject matter covered herein. It is sold with the clear understanding that the Publisher is not engaged in rendering legal or any other professional services. If legal or any other expert assistance is required, the services of a competent person should be sought. FROM A DECLARATION OF PARTICIPANTS JOINTLY ADOPTED BY A COMMITTEE OF THE AMERICAN BAR ASSOCIATION AND A COMMITTEE OF PUBLISHERS.

Additional color graphics may be available in the e-book version of this book.

LIBRARY OF CONGRESS CATALOGING-IN-PUBLICATION DATA
Salem, Abdel-Fattah Z. M.
Guidelines for writing and preparing a manuscript for international
publication / Abdel-Fattah Z. M. Salem...[et al.].
p. cm.
Includes bibliographical references and index.
ISBN 978-1-61761-799-7 (softcover)
1. Technical writing. I. Title.
T11.S25 2010
808'.0666--dc22
2010033111

Published by Nova Science Publishers, Inc. † New York

CONTENTS

PREFACE

Research results prepared for publication is an integral part of a researcher's professional life. As professionals engaged in some aspect of wildlife science, a significant amount of your time will be spent communicating with other professionals through writing. However, writing is not every researcher's favorite activity, and the obstacles of getting a paper published can be nerve-wracking.

This book, as a collected informations gives an introductory report on basic issues for writing and organizing scientific papers, and getting them published. The book also outlines the process of publishing research papers for international publication in journals and conference proceedings, aiming to provide interested novices with a handy introductory guide. The book deals in 140 pages with issues of writing scientific research papers, from the intent to write a paper to planning the writing for professional and international publication. The major part of this section outlines principles of paper organization. This book including five chapters, starting with a general introduction that describing the method of calculation the impact factor of the international journals that indexed in the Journal Citation Report (JCR), and follow with all manuscript principal sections (title, authors, abstract, introduction, materials and methods, results, discussion, conclusions and references).

It is effectual to follow the usual structure of scientific papers: introduction, methods, results, discussion, and conclusion. Introduction gives the review of the literature studying your problem and leads to the aim and the hypothesis of your research. The methods part contains the description of the research in detail, which enables the reader to do the research over again. Results are usually given in tables and graphs.

Discussion includes the analyses of the data received to find support or reject the hypothesis raised in introduction. The inferences are compared with the findings of other researchers and shortcomings and/or tasks for further research are pointed out.

Chapter 1

GENERAL INTRODUCTION

GOALS OF THE INTERNATIONAL PUBLICATION

1. To improve the ranking of our institute among the national and international institutions, for the international institute quality accreditation (*ISO certificate*).
2. To improve our knowledge about the new information available in our professional research work.
3. To improve our scientific activities as well as the name of the institute around the world in our professional field of research.
4. To improve our possibility of getting funds from the international foundations.

GENERAL REMARKS

The manuscript should be prepared as you wish it to appear in the journal. Formulas, tables and figures should be inserted within the text of the document as you would like them to appear.

- The manuscript should be well written and free of spelling and grammatical errors.
- Authors should be sure to run their manuscript through a grammar and spell checker to correct any errors prior to submission.
- It is important that you set your word processor according to the guidelines outlined at the bottom of this document. Setting your word

processor in this way will insure that the necessary issues are addressed.

INTERNATIONAL JOURNALS RANKING

On the international level, it is found two principal organizations or institutions for ranking the scientific journals depending on many criteria such combine industry expertise with innovative technology to deliver critical information to leading decision makers in the financial, legal, tax and accounting, scientific, healthcare and media markets, powered by the world's most trusted news organization.

Thomson Reuters, shares are listed on the New York Stock Exchange (NYSE: TRI); Toronto Stock Exchange (TSX: TRI); London Stock Exchange (LSE: TRIL); and Nasdaq (NASDAQ: TRIN). Thomson Reuters is the world's leading source of intelligent information for businesses and professionals.

Red Jasper's Center (RJC), Journal-ranking.com by the RJC which provide a brand new program to ranking more than 7,000 journals from all disciplines of according to its some definitions especially the Impact Factor (IF) depending on the *Journal Citation Reports*.

- Journal–ranking.com is perhaps the first and only online interactive journal ranking service in the world.
- The service allows users to configure their ranking interests, as well as provides a more reasonable method to evaluate a journal's impact.

JOURNAL CITATION REPORTS [1]

Journal Citation Reports (JCR) offers a systematic, objective means to critically evaluate the world's leading journals, with quantifiable, statistical information based on citation data. By compiling articles' cited references, JCR web helps to measure research influence and impact at the journal and category levels, and shows the relationship between citing and cited journals.

JCR is available in Science and Social Sciences editions. In addition, the JCR provides quantitative tools for ranking, evaluating, categorizing, and comparing journals. The *journal impact factor* (JIF) is one of these; it is a measure of the *frequency* with which the "*average article*" in a journal has been cited in a particular year or period. JIF applies only to a journal or groups of journals, but not to individual articles or individual researchers (Figure 1.1, and Figure 1.2.).

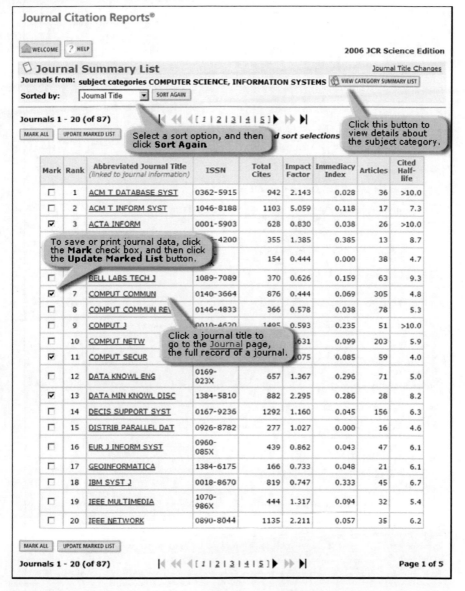

Figure 1.1. Evaluation of journals according to the Journal Citation Reports [1].

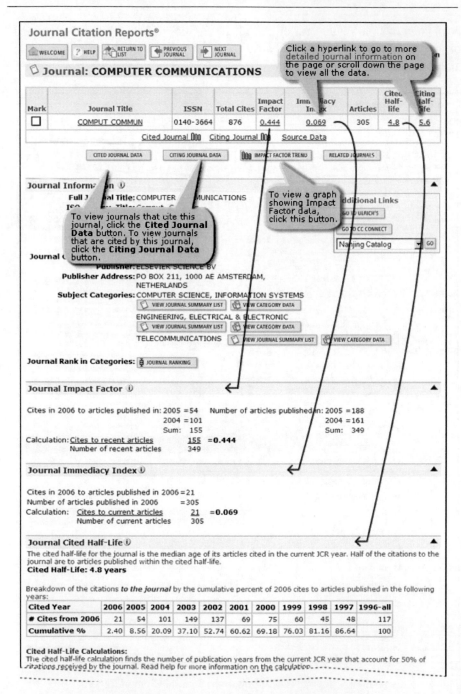

Figure 1.2. Summary and detailed information about a journal [2].

JOURNAL IMPACT FACTOR [3]

Librarians and information scientists have been evaluating journals for at least 75 years. Gross and Gross conducted a classic study of citation patterns in the '20s [4]. Others, including Estelle Brodman with her studies in the '40s of physiology journals and subsequent reviews of the process, followed this lead [5].

However, the advent of the Thomson Scientific citation indexes made it possible to do computer-compiled statistical reports not only on the output of journals but also in terms of citation frequency. And in the '60s they invented the journal "impact factor."

After using journal statistical data in-house to compile the *Science Citation Index (SCI)* for many years, Thomson Scientific began to publish JCR [6,7] in 1975 as part of the SCI and the *Social Sciences Citation Index (SSCI)* [8]. Informed and careful use of these impact data is essential. Users may be tempted to jump to ill-formed conclusions based on impact factor statistics unless several caveats are considered.

DEFINITION

Journal Impact Factor (JIF) is from JCR, a product of Thomson Institute for Scientific Information (Thomson ISI). JCR provides quantitative tools for evaluating journals and JIF is one of these. It is a measure of the frequency with which the "average article" in a journal has been cited in a given period of time.

However, JIF is frequently used as a proxy for the importance of a journal to its field. JCR [9] and the Eigenfactor [10] are tools for finding the impact of a journal or groups of journals.

The IF of a journal in a particular year is the number of citations received in the current year to articles published in the two preceding years divided by the number of articles published in the same two years. For example, *Pediatrics* has a 2006 IF of 5.012, which means that on average each of its 2004 and 2005 articles was cited 5.012 times in 2006. The IF is useful in clarifying the significance of absolute (or total) citation frequencies.

It eliminates some of the bias of such counts which favor large journals over small ones, or frequently issued journals over less frequently issued ones, and of older journals over newer ones.

Particularly in the latter case such journals have a larger citable body of literature than smaller or younger journals. All things being equal, the larger the number of previously published articles, the more often a journal will be cited [11,12].

HOW TO CALCULATE THE JIF?

The JIF for a journal is calculated based on a three-year period, and can be considered to be the average number of times published papers are cited up to two years after publication. For example, the impact factor 2010 for a journal would be calculated as follows:

A= the number of times articles published in 2008-9 were cited in indexed journals during 2010.

B= the number of articles, reviews, proceedings or notes published in 2008-9.

Impact factor 2010 = A/B

(Note that the IF 2009 will be actually published in 2010, because it could not be calculated until all of the 2010 publications had been received. IF 2010 will be published in 2011) An IF is one measure of the relative importance of a journal, individual article or scientist to science and social science literature and research.

Each index or database used to create an IF uses a different methodology and produces slightly different results, revealing the importance of using several sources to judge the true impact of a journal's or scientist's work. Included on this page is information on JIF [13] and Author Impact Factor [14]. Informed and careful use of these impact data is essential, and should be based on a thorough understanding of the methodology used to generate impact factors. There are controversial aspects of using *impact factors*:

- It is not clear whether the number of times a paper is cited measures its actual quality.
- Some databases that calculate impact factors fail to incorporate publications including textbooks, handbooks and reference books.

- Certain disciplines have low numbers of journals and usage. Therefore, one should only compare journals or researchers within the same discipline.
- Review articles normally are cited more often and therefore can skew results.
- Self-citing may also skew results.
- Some resources used to calculate impact factors have inadequate international coverage.
- Editorial policies can artificially inflate an impact factor.

HOW TO FIND THE JIF BY INDIVIDUAL JOURNAL TITLE OR BY SUBJECT GROUPINGS

1. Go to *JCR* [15].
2. Select a *JCR* edition year from dropdown list (leave view group of journals by subject category).
3. Click Submit button.
4. Select one or more subject categories (hold down control key while clicking subjects).
5. Select Journal or Category data sorts. Under View Journal Data, select Impact Factor.
6. Click Submit button.

INDIVIDUAL JOURNAL TITLE

1. Go to *JCR* [15].
2. Select a *JCR* edition year from dropdown list.
3. Click radio button to the left of 'Search for a specific journal'.
4. Click Submit button.
5. Enter journal information by complete title, ISSN, abbreviated journal title, or title word.
6. Click Search button.

In results table click individual journal title for complete information (e.g., explanations of impact factor, immediacy index, citing and cited half-life).

The JIF section in Citation Analysis with the *Web Of Science (WOS)* [16].

APPLICATIONS

There have been many innovative applications of JIF. The most common involve market research for publishers and others. But, primarily, JCR provides librarians and researchers with a tool for the management of library journal collections. In market research, the IF provides quantitative evidence for editors and publishers for positioning their journals in relation to the competition—especially others in the same subject category, in a vertical rather than a horizontal or intradisciplinary comparison. JCR data may also serve advertisers interested in evaluating the potential of a specific journal.

Perhaps the most important and recent use of impact is in the process of academic evaluation. The IF can be used to provide a gross approximation of the prestige of journals in which individuals have been published. This is best done in conjunction with other considerations such as peer review, productivity, and subject specialty citation rates.

As a tool for management of library journal collections, the IF supplies the library administrator with information about journals already in the collection and journals under consideration for acquisition. These data must also be combined with cost and circulation data to make rational decisions about purchases of journals.

The IF can be useful in all of these applications, provided the data are used sensibly. It is important to note that subjective methods can be used in evaluating journals as, for example, by interviews or questionnaires. In general, there is good agreement on the relative value of journals in the appropriate categories.

However, the JCR makes possible the realization that many journals do not fit easily into established categories. Often, the only differentiation possible between two or three small journals of average impact is price or subjective judgments such as peer review.

USING THE IMPACT FACTOR WISELY

Thomson Scientific does not depend on the IF alone in assessing the usefulness of a journal, and neither should anyone else. The IF should not be used without careful attention to the many phenomena that influence citation rates, as for example the average number of references cited in the average article. The IF should be used with informed peer review. In the case of academic evaluation for tenure it is sometimes inappropriate to use the impact of the source journal to estimate the expected frequency of a recently published article.

Again, the IF should be used with informed peer review. Citation frequencies for individual articles are quite varied. There are many artifacts that can influence a journal's impact and its ranking in journal lists, not the least of which is the inclusion of review articles or letters. This is illustrated in a study of the leading medical journals published in the *Annals of Internal Medicine* [17].

REVIEW ARTICLES

Review articles generally are cited more frequently than typical research articles because they often serve as surrogates for earlier literature, especially in journals that discourage extensive bibliographies. In the JCR system any article containing more than 100 references is coded as a review.

Articles in "review" sections of research or clinical journals are also coded as reviews, as are articles whose titles contain the word "review" or "overview." The Source Data Listing in the JCR not only provides data on the number of reviews in each journal but also provides the average number of references cited in that journal's articles.

Naturally, review journals have some of the highest impact factors. Often, the first-ranked journal in the subject category listings will be a review journal. For example, under Biochemistry, the journal topping the list is *Annual Review of Biochemistry* with an impact factor of 35.5 in 1992.

METHODS ARTICLES

It is widely believed that methods articles attract more citations than other types of articles. However, this is not in fact true. Many journals devoted entirely to methods do not achieve unusual impact. But it is true that among the most cited articles in the literature there are some super classics that give this overall impression. It should be noted that the chronological limitation on the impact calculation eliminates the bias super classics might introduce. Absolute citation frequencies are biased in this way, but, on occasion, a hot paper might affect the current impact of a journal.

VARIATION BETWEEN DISCIPLINES

Different specialties exhibit different ranges of peak impact. That is why the JCR provides subject category listings. In this way, journals may be viewed in the context of their specific field. Still, a five-year impact may be more useful to some users and can be calculated by combining the statistical data available from consecutive years of the JCR (Figure 1.3). It is rare to find that the *ranking* of a journal will change significantly within its designated category unless the journal's influence has indeed changed.

A= citations in 1992 to articles published in 1987-1991
B= articles published in 1987-1991
Five-year impact factor= A/B

Figure 1.3. Calculation of five-year impact factor; one year of citations to five years of articles.

An alternative five-year impact can be calculated based on adding citations in 1988-92 articles published in the same five-year period. And yet another is possible by selecting one or two earlier years as factor "B" above.

ITEM-BY-ITEM IMPACT

While Thomson Scientific does manually code each published source item, it is not feasible to code individually the 12 million references we process each year. Therefore, journal citation counts in JCR do not distinguish between letters, reviews, or original research. So, if a journal publishes a large number of letters, there will usually be a temporary increase in references to those letters. Letters to the *Lancet* may indeed be cited more often that letters to *JAMA* or vice versa, but the overall citation count recorded would not take this artifact into account. Detailed computerized article-by-article analyses or audits can be conducted to identify such artifacts.

CITED-ONLY JOURNALS IN THE JCR

Some of the journals listed in the JCR are not citing journals, but are cited-only journals. This is significant when comparing journals by impact factor because the self-citations from a cited-only journal are not included in its impact factor calculation. Self-citations often represent about 13% of the citations that a journal receives.

The cited-only journals with impact factors in the JCR Journal Rankings and Subject Category Listing may be ceased or suspended journals, superseded titles, or journals that are covered in the science editions of *Current Contents*, but not a citation index. Users can identify cited-only journals by checking the JCR Citing Journal Listing. Furthermore, users can establish analogous impact factors, (excluding self-citations), for the journals they are evaluating using the data given in the Citing Journal Listing (Figure 1.4 and Table 1.1 for numerical example).

A= citations in 1992 to articles published in 1990-91
B= 1992 self-citations to articles published in 1990-91
C= A - B = total citations minus self-citations to recent articles
D= number of articles published 1990-91
E= revised IF (C/D)

Figure 1.4. Calculation for impact factor revised to exclude self-citations.

Table 1.1. Calculation of impact factors without self-citations

Reproductive Systems Journals	(A/D) JCR Impact Factor	A Cites in 1992 to 1990-91 Articles	B Self-cites in 1992 to 1990-91 Articles	C (A-B) Minus Self-Cites	D Articles Published 1990-91	E (C/D) Revised Impact Factor
AM J REPROD IMMUNOL	1.931	224	54	170	116	1.466
ANIM REPROD SCI	0.701	110	23	87	157	0.554
BIOL REPROD	3.257	726	265	461	530	2.757
EUR J OBSTET GYN R B	0.449	169	19	150	376	0.399
HUM REPROD	1.328	627	*	627	472	1.328
INVERTEBR REPROD DEV	0.899	98	8	90	109	0.826
J REPROD FERTIL	2.211	1287	209	1078	582	1.852

Table 1.1. (Continued)

Reproductive Systems Journals	(A/D) JCR Impact Factor	A Cites in 1992 to 1990-91 Articles	B Self-cites in 1992 to 1990-91 Articles	C (A-B) Minus Self-Cites	D Articles Published 1990-91	E (C/D) Revised Impact Factor
J REPROD IMMUNOL	1.442	137	20	117	95	1.232
MOL REPROD DEV	2.003	597	107	490	298	1.644
OXFORD REV REPROD B	1.765	30	*	30	17	1.765
REPROD DOMEST ANIM	0.565	39	2	37	69	0.536
REPROD FERT DEVELOP	1.493	221	40	181	148	1.223
REPROD NUTR DEV	0.579	84	10	74	145	0.510
REPROD TOXICOL	0.859	79	26	53	92	0.576
SEMIN REPROD ENDOCR	0.347	25	*	25	72	0.347
SEX PLANT REPROD	1.659	136	38	98	82	1.195

* In 1992, Human Reproduction was not covered in a citation index, but has been added to the Science Citation Index (SCI) for 1993. The 1992 issue of Oxford Reviews of Reproductive Biology was not received in time to process its citations for Thomson Reuters 1992 database. Seminars in Reproductive Endocrinology is not covered in a citation index.

CALCULATION OF JIF WHEN THE TITLE CHANGE [18]

A user's knowledge of the content and history of the journal studied is very important for appropriate interpretation of impact factors. Situations such as those mentioned above and others such as title change are very important, and often misunderstood, considerations.

A title change affects the IF for two years after the change is made. The old and new titles are not unified unless the titles are in the same position alphabetically.

In the first year after the title change, the impact is not available for the new title unless the data for old and new can be unified. In the second year, the impact factor is split.

The new title may rank lower than expected and the old title may rank higher than expected because only one year of source data is included in its calculation. Title changes for the current year and the previous year are listed in the JCR guide.

UNIFIED 1992 IMPACT FACTOR CALCULATION FOR TITLE CHANGE [18]

A= 1992 citations to articles published in 1990-91 (A1 + A2)
A1= those for new title
A2= those for superseded title
B= number of articles published in 1990-91 (B1 + B2)
B1= those for new title
B2= those for superseded title

Although impact factors are based on cites to articles published in the previous two years, average citation rates can be calculated using older or longer time periods.

A base of five years may be more appropriate for journals in certain fields because the body of citations may not be large enough to make reasonable comparisons, publication schedules may be consistently late, or it may take longer than two years to disseminate and respond to published works.

TO CALCULATE A FIVE-YEAR IMPACT FACTOR [18]

1. Find the journal for which you want to calculate a five-year IF. Go to the Journal [19] page.
2. Click the IF Trend button.
3. Scroll down the page to find the number of articles published in the past five years. Add up the numbers to find the total. For example, if

you start out in JCR Science Edition 2003, you need to find the total number of articles published in 2002, 2001, 2000, 1999, and 1998.

4. Click the Return to Journal. On the Journal page, click the Cited Journal Data button to go to the Cited Journal Table.

5. Look in the All Journals row at the top of the table. Skip the first two columns (All years and JCR year). Add up the numbers in the next five columns. For example, if the JCR year is 2003, you want find the total of the numbers found in columns 2002, 2001, 2000, 1999, and 1998.

6. Divide the total number of citations found in step 5 by the total number of articles found in set How to Calculate a Unified Impact Factor.

THIS IS THE FIVE-YEAR IMPACT FACTOR [18]

If you are interested in a journal that has changed titles, split into multiple titles, or merged with another title, you may be to calculate a unified impact factor if the data are available. This can provide continuity for your journal evaluation until the new title is established.

TO UNIFY AN IMPACT FACTOR FOR A JOURNAL AFFECTED BY A TITLE CHANGE [19]

1. Print out the template at the bottom of this Help page.
2. From the Journal Title Changes [20] page, find the title of the journal and its old/new title.
3. Access the Journal [19] page for each title.
4. Scroll down the page to find the Impact Factor data.
5. Note the numbers for cites to recent articles, the number of recent articles, and the impact factor. Fill in the blanks in the template below.
6. Total the figures in columns A and B to unify the cites to recent articles and the number of recent articles.
7. Divide the unified sum of column A by the unified sum of column B to to find the unified impact factor (column C).

	A Current year cites to articles published in year-1 and year-2	B Number of articles published in year-1 and year-2	C Current year Impact Factor column A/column B
All old title(s)			
New title			
Unified (old + new)			

Examples of the JIF of some international journals

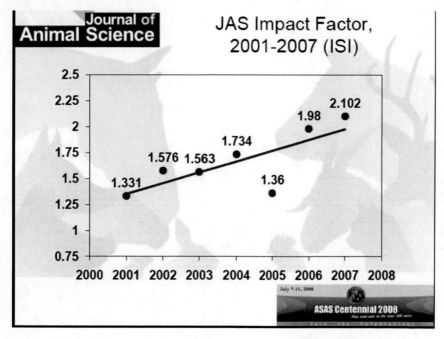

Figure 1.5. 2008 Journal Impact Factor from Journal of Animal Science [54].

EIGENFACTOR [18]

Eigenfactor ranks and maps scientific knowledge:

- Ranks journals similar to *Google* ranking of websites. It uses the structure of the entire network (instead of purely local citation information) to evaluate the importance of each journal.

- Measures journal price as well as citation influence. The Cost-Effectiveness Search orders journals by a measure of the value of the dollar they provide.
- Ranks scholarly journals as well as newspapers, theses, popular magazines, etc.
- Adjusts for citation differences across disciplines, allowing for better comparison across research areas.
- Calculations are based on the citations received over a 5-year period vs 2 years in *JCR*.
- Available free of charge on the web [25].

How to find the Eigenfactor?

1. Go to eigenfactor.org.
2. Search for a single journal name or choose a subject category.
3. Select a year.
4. Click Search.

Note: Cost effective (searches by category) and advanced search (searches by Thomson JCR subject categories, publisher, and other fields) are also available.

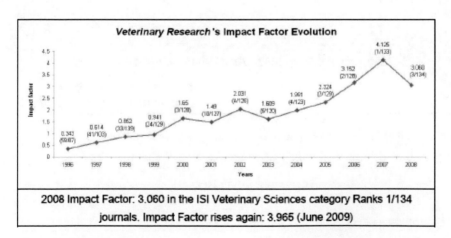

Figure 1.6. 2008 Journal Impact Factor from Veterinary Research.

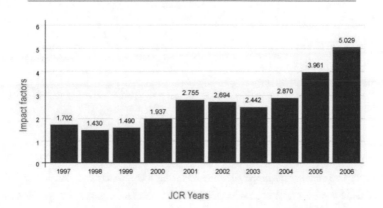

Figure 1.7. 2007 Journal Impact Factor from Bulletin of the World Health Organization [21].

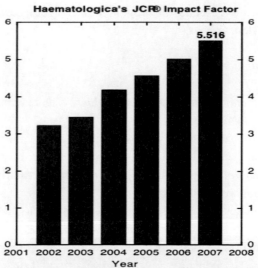

The 2007 JCR Science Edition has just been published. The 2007 JCR Impact Factor of Haematologica is equal to 5.516. The graph illustrates the journal's impact Factor trend since 2002 [22].

Figure 1.8. 2008 Journal Impact Factor from Haematologica.

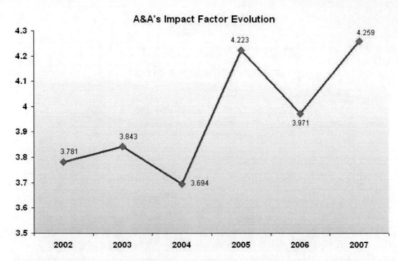

The 2007 Astronomy & Astrophysics impact factor: 4.259 which was released on 18 June 2008 by the Journal Citation Reports, ISI Web of Knowledge. Astronomy & Astrophysics articles were the second most cited with 76,647 citations in 2007.

Figure 1.8. 2007 Journal Impact Factor from Astronomy and Astrophysics [23].

Get more information about impact factors [24]. The following is some general information about the Eigenfactor. Eigenfactor ranks and maps scientific knowledge:

Why eigenfactor? [26]

1. *Eigenfactor* scores and *Article Influence* scores rank journals much as *Google* ranks websites.
- Scholarly references join journals together in a vast network of citations. Our algorithms use the structure of the entire network (instead of purely local citation information) to evaluate the importance of each journal.
2. Eigenfactor.org reports journal prices as well as citation influence.
- In collaboration with journalprices.com [27], *Eigenfactor.org* provides information about price and value for thousands of scholarly periodicals. While the *Eigenfactor Scores* and *Article Influence Scores* do not incorporate price information directly, the Cost-Effectiveness Search [28] orders journals by a measure of the value per dollar that they provide.
3. Eigenfactor.org contains 115,000 reference items.

- *Eigenfactor.org*not only ranks scholarly journals in the natural and social sciences, but also lists newsprint, PhD theses, popular magazines and more. In so doing, it more fairly values those journals bridging the gap between the social and natural sciences.

4. *Eigenfactor* scores and *Article Influence* scores adjust for citation differences across disciplines.

- Different disciplines have different standards for citation and different time scales on which citations occur. The average article in a leading cell biology journal might receive 10-30 citations within two years; the average article in leading mathematics journal would do very well to receive 2 citations over the same period. By using the whole citation network, our algorithm automatically accounts for these differences and allows better comparison across research areas.

5. *Eigenfactor* scores and *Article Influence* scores rely on 5-year citation data.

- In many research areas, articles are not frequently cited until several years after publication. Therefore, measures that only look at citations in the first two years after publication can be misleading. The *Eigenfactor* score and the *Article Influence* score is calculated based on the citations received over a five year period.

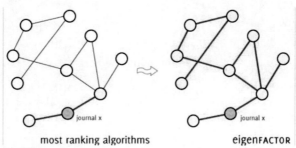

most ranking algorithms   eigenFACTOR

©2009 Carl Bergstrom

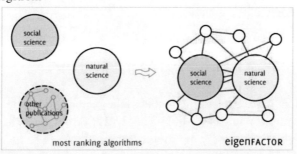

most ranking algorithms   eigenFACTOR

©2009 Carl Bergstrom

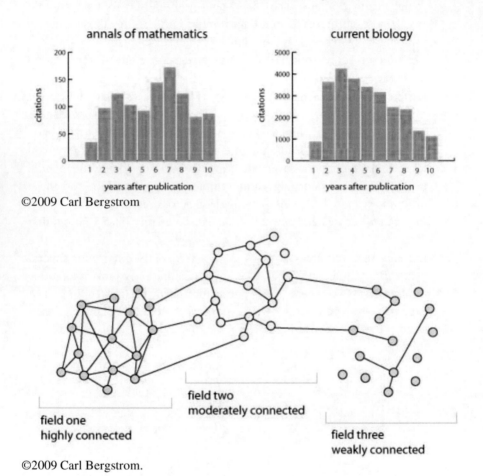

number of citations vs. time in years

©2009 Carl Bergstrom

©2009 Carl Bergstrom.

6. *Eigenfactor* scores and *Article Influence* scores are completely free and completely searchable [28].

AUTHOR IMPACT FACTOR

The Author impact factor calculates the scientific value of a given researcher or author. You can try the h-index [29] or compile cited references [30] by using Web of Science [31] or Google Scholar [32].

H-INDEX [33]

The h-index quantifies the actual scientific productivity and the apparent impact of the scientist. The h-index is based on the author's most cited papers and the number of citations they have received from other articles.

"A scientist has index h if h of his/her Np papers have at least h citations each, and the other (Np − h) papers have no more than h citations each" [34]. An h-index of 16 means, for example, that a researcher has published 16 papers that each had at least 16 citations. Therefore, the h-index reflects both the number of articles as well as the number of citations per article.

How to find the H-index of an individual author in Web of Science [33]

1. Go to Web of Science from the Reference page or Databases list.
2. Enter author's name and be sure the pull-down box indicates Author.
3. Click Search.
4. Refine Results by subject areas or other criteria if desired.
5. Click 'Create Citation Report' link (right side of window, just above results list).
6. The Citation Report lists the h-index near the top right of the page.

CITED REFERENCES

Cited references make it possible to find other documents that are related by topic or subject to the original document. Cited references (references that cite an individual article) may be used to measure the usage and impact of a cited work. Note that cited references can be influenced by author self-citing or publishing in an open access journal. Citation analysis, which involves counting how many times a paper or researcher is cited, assumes that influential scientists and important works are cited more often than others.

WEB OF SCIENCE CITED REFERENCES [38]

Cited Reference Search is one of the features in the WOS database. The number in the Citing Articles column in WOS indicates the number of times the reference has been cited in all years of WOS, regardless of how many years you are searching. Note that Citing Article references may not include all the known citations of the paper, just those in journals covered by WOS.

How to Perform a WoS Cited Reference Search

1. Enter the name of the primary Cited Author and the Cited Year or a limited range of years of a Cited Work, and then click Search [35].
2. If you retrieve too many hits, return to the form and add the abbreviated title of a Cited Work.
3. After you click Search, you will see references from the citation index that contain the cited author/cited work data you entered. You can note how many times the article or work has been cited in the Citing Articles column.
4. Select references by checking the box to the left of each reference you want.
5. To retrieve these citing articles, click Finish Search. You have now retrieved the records of articles that cite the author/reference you selected.
6. Clicking on Analyze Results allows you to view rankings of the authors, journals, etc. for your set of results.

For further help:
Cited Reference Searching in the Web of Science [36].
Citation Analysis with the Web of Science, PartII: Cited Ref Search, Author Finder and Impact Factor [37].

GOOGLE SCHOLAR (BETA) CITED REFERENCES [38]

Google Scholar (GS) covers peer-reviewed papers, theses, books, abstracts, and other scholarly literature from all broad areas of research and from a wide variety of academic publishers and professional societies, as well as scholarly articles available across the web.

Each GS search result contains bibliographic information, such as the title, author names, and source of publication.

At the end of the search result is a "Cited by" link, which will display a list of articles and documents that have cited the document, originally retrieved in the search. Note that this only includes resources indexed by GS. There have been some criticisms of *Google Scholar* Cited References, such as:

- GS includes some non-scholarly citations.
- It is not clear exactly which scholarly resources are included in GS.
- GS does not perform well for older publications.
- GS is a beta product and may change at any time.
- GS is not updated as often as WOS.

How to find Cited References in Google Scholar:

1. Go to GS [39].
2. Enter search terms, such as an individual author or a particular article citation.
3. Look for the "Cited by" link at the bottom of the citation.
4. Click on the "Cited by" link to retrieve citations to the original resource.

CITATION-BASED AND DESCRIPTOR-BASED SEARCH STRATEGIES [40]

In the last two essays, we explained citation indexing and its usefulness in navigating the research literature [41,42]. In this essay we will explore the possibilities of retrieval using key word and cited reference searches. The *Science Citation Index* (SCI) was originally designed as an alternative approach for retrieval of relevant information; but the concept of relevance is not as simple as it sounds. Relevance, like beauty, is in the eye of the beholder.

Regardless of the initial approach to a search—whether through a key word index or through a citation index—only the citation index will easily permit retrieval of subsequent papers that refer to a specific paper or book that the user has deemed "relevant". Systems like SCI rely on the judgment of authors and referees who choose references for published papers. In systems like MEDLINE, the judgment of indexers determines the terms used, and the systems are based on the thesaurus called Medical Subject Headings (MeSH). Since human effort is involved, there is always the problem of consistency from one article to another. And, in traditional indexing, there are economic limitations to the number of headings that can be assigned to each new article. In any case, thesauri have innate problems in dealing with active, fast-moving fields in which the terminology changes rapidly. Following the example set by the online version of SCI on DIALOG back in 1972, MEDLINE adopted title word indexing several years ago to partially offset this difficulty. Nevertheless, a major complaint about MeSH indexing is that in many cases the generally broader terms retrieve too much information. However, skilled users of MEDLINE can use the standard list of subheadings available to reduce retrieval to a more manageable number of hits. Thus, as an example, compare a search on cancer with a search on cancer epidemiology.

COMPARATIVE STUDIES

Studies comparing citation-based retrieval with the use of MeSH have been conducted, including an early study by Spencer. She found that in the beginning of a search, use of *SCI* provided results in a more rapid and efficient manner [43]. But to obtain a more comprehensive result, back-up with Index Medicus was necessary. Later studies, including McCain's [44], focus on the complementary aspects of the two systems. McCain found that retrieval by descriptor-based and citation-based searches does not significantly overlap [44]. Depending on the subject matter, there are topics for which the use of either a single word or citation may capture 90% or more of the "relevant" literature. While a search on a specific disease can be run by a key word, it is almost impossible to use key words to retrieve every paper that uses or modifies a method or theory.

McCain's study considered 11 search topics—such as interpersonal problem solving, rehabilitation and therapy for aphasia following stroke, and the classical conditioning of drug effects—which were suggested b y researchers.

McCain also asked the researchers to identify relevant older contributions that were likely to be cited in more recent work. In either case, the search results were evaluated in terms of relevance and novelty. Interpreting the results, McCain suggests that "subsets of both literatures may be relevant to a given researcher's information needs, serving related rather than identical functions" [44].

RELEVANCE [44]

Relevance is a vast subject that deserves a discussion in its own right. Nevertheless, most evaluation studies designed to measure relevance do not capture the significance of "being cited." If you specifically ask whether a particular author or paper has been cited, then any citing paper is relevant. However, a paper on topic A could be cited in a paper on topic B, but the latter might not be deemed relevant in a traditional comparison of A and B (or other papers C and D) since they may not be terminologically connected.

There are countless examples in which two or more subsequent articles will cite a designated paper, but the various citing titles will not necessarily overlap in the terms used to describe their content—neither in the title nor in the key words or abstracts. Whether the citation-based common thread is methodological, theoretical, or otherwise, only the searcher can determine its relevance. Indeed, it is frequently the unexpected connection that may prove to be most relevant—that is, the most interesting. This will vary with the purpose of the search. That is why I often contrast the needs of information recovery with those of information discovery.

NOVELTY

If your primary aim is to find the known literature on a topic, then precision of search may be all-important. But if you are interested in finding previously unknown connections, then the system must facilitate your ability to do this without retrieving everything that is published. In traditional searching, this is done by using boolean combinations of terms.

TIMING

One of the problems with traditional indexing is the inherent delay introduced by using human indexers. To overcome this problem, many journals have implemented author key word indexing. Unfortunately, only about 25% of published articles contain author assigned key words. Thomson Scientific uses these to augment its unique capability to provide derivative indexing called *KeyWords Plus.*

Key Words Plus

KeyWords Plus is called derivative indexing because the terms are derived from the titles of articles cited by the author of the article being indexed [45]. *KeyWords Plus* augments traditional key word or title retrieval to a varied extent—anywhere from 10% to over 100%. For example, using *Current*

Contents on Diskette, you can search on an article such as "The spectrum of autoimmune thyroid disease with uticaria" from *Clinical Endocrinology,* and find that the key words UTICARIA, VASCULITIS, THYROID DISEASE, and HASHIMOTO THYROIDITIS are expanded to include the additional *KeyWords Plus* terms ASSOCIATION and ANGIODERMA. Again, the user is the ultimate filter. When *KeyWords Plus* is used in a weekly or monthly file, as with *Current Contents*, you can readily filter out the noise from the music. On the other hand, doing an annual search may require further refinement, as mentioned above, by combining one or more words and cited references.

RED JASPAR'S CENTER [46]

To check a journal ranking on the world you will find the following table some definitions:

No.	The row of the record in the result table
Journal	The name of the journal
Rank	The rank of journal among all journals based on PII
JII	Journal Influence Index, the score of the journal calculated by our method, the bigger more impactful
PII	Paper Influence Index, the JII divided by article number multiplied by 1000
B2(2005)	The average number of citations received by papers published in the journal in the 2 preceding years before 2005 (2004, 2003) from all the papers published in 2005. This is also commonly known as the ISI IF
B4(2005)	The average number of citations received by papers published in the journal in the 4 preceding years before 2005 (2004, 2003, 2002, 2001) from all the papers published in 2005
B6(2005)	The average number of citations received by papers published in the journal in the 6 preceding years before 2005 (2004, 2003, 2002, 2001, 2000, 1999) from all the papers published in 2005.

Table 1.2. Example for the Journal Ranking in our field of Agriculture Dairy and Animal Science

No.	Journal	Rank	JII	PII	B2	B4	B6
1	JOURNAL OF ANIMAL SCIENCE	1687	24.47	80.55	2.68	3.15	3.27
2	GENETICS SELECTION EVOLUTION	1797	3.26	75.00	3.01	4.21	3.53
3	ANIMAL GENETICS	2148	5.55	60.67	4.51	4.22	4.33
4	JOURNAL OF DAIRY SCIENCE	2451	23.01	51.22	4.27	4.57	4.50
5	APPLIED ANIMAL BEHAVIOUR SCIENCE	2497	6.28	50.02	2.75	3.10	3.27
6	POULTRY SCIENCE	2625	12.59	46.45	3.40	3.39	3.44
7	JOURNAL OF DAIRY RESEARCH	2796	2.91	42.45	3.04	3.68	3.55
8	CANADIAN JOURNAL OF ANIMAL SCIENCE	3584	1.78	29.16	1.66	1.85	1.89
9	DOMESTIC ANIMAL ENDOCRINOLOGY	3859	1.61	25.45	2.81	4.29	4.02
10	BRITISH POULTRY SCIENCE	3955	3.06	24.13	1.54	1.90	2.14
11	LIVESTOCK PRODUCTION SCIENCE	3967	3.85	23.94	2.50	2.61	2.68

Table 1.2 (Continued)

12	JOURNAL OF ANIMAL BREEDING AND GENETICS	4089	1.12	22.47	1.92	1.87	1.82
13	ANIMAL REPRODUCTION SCIENCE	4145	2.77	21.62	4.03	3.71	4.14
14	ANIMAL SCIENCE	4217	2.07	20.78	1.88	2.45	2.67
15	ACTA AGRICULTURAE SCANDINAVICA SECTION A-ANIMAL SC...	4426	0.39	18.32	0.98	1.84	1.86
16	WORLDS POULTRY SCIENCE JOURNAL	4443	0.69	18.22	2.01	2.40	2.28
17	ANIMAL FEED SCIENCE AND TECHNOLOGY	4468	2.60	17.87	2.16	2.41	2.68
18	ANIMAL BIOTECHNOLOGY	4774	0.25	14.66	1.53	2.71	2.13
19	AUSTRALIAN JOURNAL OF DAIRY TECHNOLOGY	5212	0.48	10.99	1.01	1.26	1.15
20	TROPICAL GRASSLANDS	5294	0.26	10.45	0.30	0.38	0.40
21	REPRODUCTION IN DOMESTIC ANIMALS	5553	0.61	8.75	3.45	3.09	2.59
22	ARCHIVES OF ANIMAL NUTRITION	5700	0.30	7.83	1.83	1.93	1.66
23	JOURNAL OF APPLIED POULTRY RESEARCH	5857	0.55	6.89	1.55	1.60	1.57

24	AVIAN AND POULTRY BIOLOGY REVIEWS	5882	0.14	6.70	1.17	1.14	1.17
25	ARCHIV FUR TIERZUCHT-ARCHIVES OF ANIMAL BREEDING	5909	0.36	6.47	0.93	1.02	1.03
26	JOURNAL OF REPRODUCTION AND DEVELOPMENT	6007	0.40	5.82	3.98	2.74	2.15
27	SMALL RUMINANT RESEARCH	6062	0.80	5.49	1.47	1.57	1.64
28	ARCHIV FUR GEFLUGELKUNDE	6190	0.19	4.77	0.52	0.81	0.89
29	SOUTH AFRICAN JOURNAL OF ANIMAL SCIENCE	6279	0.11	4.33	1.49	1.10	1.05
30	ANIMAL RESEARCH	6593	0.11	2.84	1.55	1.85	1.24
31	PRODUCTIONS ANIMALES	6615	0.08	2.69	0.72	0.84	0.83
32	ZUCHTUNGSKUNDE	6724	0.08	2.21	0.52	0.69	0.68
33	JOURNAL OF ANIMAL AND FEED SCIENCES	6876	0.20	1.53	0.61	0.70	0.59
34	JOURNAL OF APPLIED ANIMAL RESEARCH	6905	0.08	1.39	0.25	0.34	0.33
35	ASIAN-AUSTRALASIAN JOURNAL OF ANIMAL SCIENCES	6933	0.36	1.26	1.67	1.37	1.08

Table 1.2 (Continued)

36	INDIAN JOURNAL OF ANIMAL SCIENCES	7041	0.25	0.86	0.24	0.30	0.33
37	CUBAN JOURNAL OF AGRICULTURAL SCIENCE	7050	0.03	0.81	0.68	1.16	1.09
38	CZECH JOURNAL OF ANIMAL SCIENCE	7067	0.05	0.70	0.49	0.61	0.58
39	REVISTA BRASILEIRA DE ZOOTECNIA-BRAZILIAN JOURNAL ...	7105	0.07	0.50	1.06	1.76	1.86
40	Rangeland Ecology and Management	7151	0.01	0.19			
41	WOOL TECHNOLOGY AND SHEEP BREEDING	7230	N/A	N/A	0.05	0.19	0.19
42	JOURNAL OF RANGE MANAGEMENT	7252	N/A	N/A	1.40	1.74	1.82
43	ANNALES DE ZOOTECHNIE	7489	N/A	N/A			
44	ANNALS OF ARID ZONE	7494	N/A	N/A			
45	ALL JOURNALS	7886	N/A	N/A			

Chapter 2

TITLE AND ABSTRACT

A major goal of this chapter is the development of effective technical writing skills. To help you become an accomplished writer, you will prepare several research papers based upon the studies completed in lab. Our research papers are not typical "lab reports". In a teaching lab a lab report might be nothing more than answers to a set of questions. Such an assignment hardly represents the kind of writing you might be doing in your eventual career [47].

Written and oral communications skills are probably the most universal qualities sought by graduate and professional schools as well as by employers. You alone are responsible for developing such skills to a high level [47].

WHY A SCIENTIFIC FORMAT OF THE PAPER?

The scientific format may seem confusing for the beginning science writer due to its rigid structure which is so different from writing in the humanities. One reason for using this format is that it is a means of efficiently communicating scientific findings to the broad community of scientists in a uniform manner. Another reason, perhaps more important than the first, is that this format allows the paper to be read at several different levels. For example, many people skim Titles to find out what information is available on a subject. Others may read only titles and Abstracts. Those wanting to go deeper may look at the Tables and Figures in the Results, and so on. The take home point here is that the scientific format helps to insure that at whatever level a person reads your paper (beyond title skimming), they will likely get the key results and conclusions [48].

RESOURCES FOR LEARNING TECHNICAL WRITING [47]

Before you begin your first writing assignment, please consult all of the following resources, in order to gain the most benefit from the experience.

- General form of a typical research article
- Specific guidelines (if any) for the assignment – see the write-ups on individual lab studies
- McMillan, VE. "Writing Papers in the Biological Sciences, Third Ed." New York: Bedford/St. Martin's, 2001. ISBN 0-312-25857-7 (REQUIRED for Bios 211, 311, recommended for other science courses that include writing)
- Writing portfolio examples [49]

As you polish up your writing skills please make use of the following resources

- Instructions feedback on previous assignments
- Common errors in student research papers [50]
- Selected writing rules (somewhat less serious than the other resources) [51]

For Biosciences majors the general guidelines apply to future course work, as can be seen by examining the guidelines for the advanced experimental sciences research paper [52]. Instructions for authors from the Journal of Biological Chemistry editorial board may be helpful as well. Their statement of editorial policies and practices [53] may give you an idea of how material makes its way into the scientific literature.

GENERAL FORM OF A RESEARCH PAPER [47]

An objective of organizing a research paper is to allow people to read your work selectively. When I research a topic, I may be interested in just the methods, a specific result, the interpretation, or perhaps I just want to see a summary of the paper to determine if it is relevant to my study. To this end, many journals require the following sections, submitted in the order listed, each section to start on a new page. There are variations of course. Some journals call for a combined results and discussion, for example, or include materials and methods after the body of the paper. The well known journal *Science* does away with separate sections altogether, except for the abstract.

Your papers are to adhere to the form and style required for the Journal of Biological Chemistry, requirements that are shared by many journals in the life sciences.

GENERAL STYLE

Specific editorial requirements for submission of a manuscript will always supercede instructions in these general guidelines [47].

1) To make a paper readable
- Print or type using a 12 point standard font, such as Times, Geneva, Bookman, etc.
- Text should be double spaced on 8 1/2" x 11" paper with 1 inch margins, single sided
- Number pages consecutively
- Start each new section on a new page
- Adhere to recommended page limits

2) Mistakes to avoid
- Placing a heading at the bottom of a page with the following text on the next page (insert a page break!)
- Dividing a table or figure - confine each figure/table to a single page
- Submitting a paper with pages out of order

3) In all sections of your paper
- Use normal prose including articles ("a", "the," etc.)
- Stay focused on the research topic of the paper
- Use paragraphs to separate each important point (except for the abstract)
- Indent the first line of each paragraph
- Present your points in logical order
- Use present tense to report well accepted facts - for example, 'the grass is green'
- Use past tense to describe specific results - for example, 'When weed killer was applied, the grass was brown'

- Avoid informal wording, don't address the reader directly, and don't use jargon, slang terms, or superlatives
- Avoid use of superfluous pictures - include only those figures necessary to presenting results

MANUSCRIPT PRINCIPAL SECTIONS[48]

Most journal-style scientific papers are subdivided into the following sections: Title, Authors and Affiliation, Abstract, Introduction, Methods, Results, Discussion, Acknowledgments, and Literature Cited, which parallel the experimental process. This is the system we will use. To below describes the style, content, and format associated with each section [48]. The sections appear in a journal style paper in the following prescribed order:

Question	Response (in the paper section)
What did I do in a nutshell?	Abstract
What is the problem?	Introduction
How did I solve the problem?	Materials and Methods
What did I find out?	Results
What does it mean?	Discussion
Who helped me out?	Acknowledgments (*optional*)
Whose work did I refer to?	Literature Cited
Extra Information	Appendices (*optional*)

SECTION HEADINGS [48]

Main Section Headings: Each main section of the paper begins with a heading which should be *capitalized*, *centered* at the beginning of the section, and *double spaced* from the lines above and below. *Do not underline the section heading OR put a colon at the end. Subheadings:* When your paper reports on more than one experiment, use subheadings to help organize the presentation. Subheadings should be *capitalized* (first letter in each word), *left justified,* and either *bold italics* or *underlined*.

Example of a main section heading: INTRODUCTION
Example of a subheading: *Effects of light intensity on the rate of electron*

VERY IMPORTANT REMARK/S

All sections of the paper should be writing and prepare according to the guidelines of the scientific journal.

Each journal has specific guidelines for writing the all paper sections. Example: Instructions to authors of Journal of Animal Science (REVISED 2010) [54]

The Instructions for Authors to the *Journal of Animal Science* (*JAS*) is divided into 2 sections:

(I) Manuscript Preparation, which gives the Style and Form to be used by authors in the preparation of manuscripts; and

(II) Policies and Procedures of *JAS*, which provides details concerning the mission of *JAS*, contact information, care and use of animals, the types of articles accepted by *JAS*, submitting manuscripts to *JAS* (including copyright policies), the review procedures and policies, and papers in press, author proofs, and publication charges.

I. MANUSCRIPT PREPARATION (STYLE AND FORM)

The most important thing you can do as you prepare your manuscript is to consult a recent issue of *JAS* in terms of the acceptable format for headings, title page, Abstract, Key words, Introduction, Materials and Methods, Results, Discussion (or combined Results and Discussion), Literature Cited, and tables and figures (including figure captions), which are described in more detail below. Failure to adhere to the style and form will result in immediate rejection of the manuscript.

General. Papers must be written in English and must use the American spelling and usage as well as standard scientific usage, as given in the following online resources:

· For anatomical nomenclature, consult the current *Nomina Anatomica Veterinaria* (http://www.wava-amav.org/Downloads/nav_2005.pdf).

Manuscripts should be prepared double-spaced in Microsoft Word, with lines and pages numbered consecutively, using Times New Roman font at 12 points. Special characters (e.g., Greek and symbols) should be inserted using the symbols palette available in this font. Complex equations should be entered using Math-Type or an equation editor. Tables and figures should be placed in separate sections at the end of the manuscript (not placed in the text). Authors should prepare their manuscript in Microsoft Word and upload the manuscripts using the fewest files possible to facilitate the review and editing processes.

Manuscripts should contain the following sections (Appendices or On-Line Only Data Supplements, described below, are optional), in this order:

Title Page. The title page includes a running head (the first word only and any proper nouns capitalized and no more than 45 characters plus spaces); the title (only the first word and any proper nouns capitalized, as brief as possible, and including the species involved); names of authors (e.g., T. E. Smith; no title, positions, or degrees) and institutions, including the city, state or country (all with first letters capitalized), and ZIP or postal code. Affiliations are footnoted using the symbols *, †, ‡, §, #, ||, ¶ and are placed below the author names. Footnotes on the first page (present address, and e-mail address of the corresponding author) are referenced by superscript numbers. Acknowledgments,

TITLE AND AUTHORS

Manuscript Title (in the First Page of the Manuscript) Conditions

- The manuscript title should use specific, unambiguous descriptive words that will ensure electronic retrieval
- The title should be gives and general idea about the research work done

- The scientific name should be write in the correct form (*Acacia saligna* not ACACIA SALIGNA or *Acacia Saligna*) this is very important notice
- Use word substitutes for formulas, symbols, superscripts, Greek letters, or other non-alphabetical symbols in the title
- If your title contains symbols or non-Roman letters, please suggest appropriate translations using Roman letters and provide them as keywords

TITLE PAGE

Select an informative title as illustrated in the examples in your writing portfolio example package. Include the name(s) and address(es) of all authors, and date submitted. "Biology lab #1" would not be an informative title, for example.

AUTHORS AND ADDRESS

Your paper should begin with a *Title* that succinctly describes the *contents* of the paper.

Use descriptive words that you would associate strongly with the content of your paper: the molecule studied, the organism used or studied, the treatment, the location of a field site, the response measured, etc.

A majority of readers will find your paper via electronic database searches and those search engines key on words found in the title.

- The *title* should be centered at the top of page 1 (DO NOT use a title page - it is a waste of paper for our purposes); *the title is NOT underlined or italicized.*
- The *authors' names* (PI or primary author first) and *institutional affiliation* are *double-spaced from and centered below* the title.
  When more than two authors, the names are separated by commas except for the last which is separated from the previous name by the word "and".

The title is not a section, but it is necessary and important. The title should be short and unambiguous, yet be an adequate description of the work.

A general rule-of-thumb is that the title should contain the *key words describing the work* presented. Remember that the title becomes the basis for most on-line computer searches - if your title is insufficient, few people will find or read your paper.

For example, in a paper reporting on an experiment involving dosing mice with the sex hormone estrogen and watching for a certain kind of courtship behavior, *a poor title would be: Secondary Compounds.*

Why? It is very general, and could be referring to any of a number of Secondary compounds.

A better title would be: The effects of biological treatment on secondary compounds extracted from tree leaves.

Why? Because the key words identify a specific behavior, a modifying agent, and the experimental treatment. If possible, give the key result of the study in the title, as seen in the first example.

ELSEVIER

Available online at www.sciencedirect.com

SCIENCE @ DIRECT®

Animal Feed Science and Technology
127 (2006) 251–267

ANIMAL FEED
SCIENCE AND
TECHNOLOGY

www.elsevier.com/locate/anifeedsci

Nutritive evaluations of some browse tree foliages during the dry season: Secondary compounds, feed intake and *in vivo* digestibility in sheep and goats

A.Z.M. Salem [a,*], M.Z.M. Salem [b], M.M. El-Adawy [a], P.H. Robinson [c]

[a] Department of Animal Production, Faculty of Agriculture (El-Shatby),
Alexandria University, Alexandria, Egypt
[b] Department of Timber Trees and Wood Technology, Faculty of Agriculture (El-Shatby),
Alexandria University, Alexandria, Egypt
[c] Department of Animal Science, University of California, Davis, CA 95616-8521, USA

Received 26 April 2005; received in revised form 29 August 2005; accepted 8 September 2005

Example 1.

Available online at www.sciencedirect.com

SCIENCE @ DIRECT®

Animal Feed Science and Technology
123–124 (2005) 67–79

ELSEVIER

ANIMAL FEED
SCIENCE AND
TECHNOLOGY

www.elsevier.com/locate/anifeedsci

Impact of season of harvest on in vitro gas production and dry matter degradability of *Acacia saligna* leaves with inoculum from three ruminant species

Abdel-Fattah Z.M. Salem *

Department of Animal Production, Faculty of Agriculture (El-Shatby), Alexandria University, Alexandria, Egypt

Example 2.

Animal Feed Science and Technology 155 (2010) 206–212

Contents lists available at ScienceDirect

Animal Feed Science and Technology

journal homepage: www.elsevier.com/locate/anifeedsci

ELSEVIER

Short communication

Effect of season on chemical composition and *in situ* degradability in cows and in adapted and unadapted goats of three Mexican browse species

L.M. Camacho[a], R. Rojo[a,*], A.Z.M. Salem[a,b], F.D. Provenza[c], G.D. Mendoza[d], F. Avilés[a], O.D. Montañez-Valdez[e]

[a] Centro Universitario UAEM-Temascaltepec, Universidad Autónoma del Estado de México, km 67.5 Carr. Toluca-Tejupilco, Estado de México, C.P. 51300, Mexico
[b] Department of Animal Production, Faculty of Agriculture (El-Shatby), Alexandria University, Egypt
[c] Department of Wildland Resources, Utah State University, Logan, UT 84322-5230, USA
[d] Universidad Autónoma Metropolitana, Unidad Xochimilco, México, Calzada del Hueso 1100, D.F., C.P. 04970, Mexico
[e] Centro Universitario del Sur de la Universidad de Guadalajara (CUSUR-UDG), Mexico

Example 3.

STRATEGY FOR WRITING TITLE [55]

The Title will probably be written earlier, but is often modified once the final form of the paper clearly known.

Conditions

Should be write according to the guidelines of the scientific journal and should be add star (*) with the corresponding author or authors of the paper.

ABSTRACT OR SUMMARY AND KEYWORDS

Abstract

Writing an efficient abstract is hard work, but will repay you with increased impact on the world by enticing people to read your publications. Make sure that all the components of a good abstract are included in the next one you write [56].

Whereas the Title can only make the simplest statement about the content of your article, the Abstract allows you to elaborate more on each major aspect of the paper. The length of your Abstract should be kept to about 200-300 words maximum (a typical standard length for journals.) Limit your statements concerning each segment of the paper (i.e. purpose, methods, results, etc.) to two or three sentences, if possible. The Abstract helps readers decide whether they want to read the rest of the paper, or it may be the only part they can obtain via electronic literature searches or in published abstracts. Therefore, enough key information (e.g., summary results, observations, trends, etc.) must be included to make the Abstract useful to someone who may to reference your work [48]. Because on-line search databases typically contain only abstracts, it is vital to write a complete but concise description of your work to entice potential readers into obtaining a copy of the full paper. This article describes how to write a good computer architecture abstract for both conference and journal papers. Writers should follow a checklist consisting of: motivation, problem statement, approach, results, and conclusions. Following this checklist should increase the chance of people taking the time to obtain and read your complete paper [56].

Conditions

The abstract or summary:
- Should not have the manuscript details.
- Should have the idea about the objectives, materials and methods used a short description of the very important results obtained.
- Should have a general conclusion from the results experiment done.
- It could have from 200 to 500 words.
- You need also to write an abstract at the time to submit it to the symposia or international meeting.

Now that the use of on-line publication databases is prevalent, writing a really good abstract has become even more important than it was a decade ago. Abstracts have always served the function of "selling" your work. But now, instead of merely convincing the reader to keep reading the rest of the attached paper, an abstract must convince the reader to leave the comfort of an office and go hunt down a copy of the article from a library (or worse, obtain one after a long wait through inter-library loan). In a business context, an "executive summary" is often the *only* piece of a report read by the people who matter; and it should be similar in content if not tone to a journal paper abstract [56]. An abstract is a short summary of your completed research. If done well, it makes the reader want to learn more about your research [57].

The Abstract is always the last section written because it is a concise summary of the entire paper and should include a clear statement of your aims, a brief description of the methods, the key findings, and your interpretation of the key results [58]. An abstract summarizes, in one paragraph (usually), the major aspects of the entire paper in the following prescribed sequence:

- The *question(s) you investigated* (or purpose), (from Introduction)
  - State the purpose very clearly in the first or second sentence
- The experimental design and methods used, (from Methods)
  - Clearly express the basic design of the study
  - Name or briefly describe the basic methodology used without going into excessive detail-be sure to indicate the key techniques used
- The major findings including key quantitative results, or trends (from Results)

o   Report those results which answer the questions you were asking
o   Identify trends, relative change or differences, etc.
o   A brief summary of your *interpretations* and *conclusions*, (from Discussion)
o   Clearly state the implications of the answers your results gave you

These are the basic components of an abstract in any discipline [57]

1.   Motivation/problem statement: Why do we care about the problem? What practical, scientific, theoretical or artistic gap is your research filling?
2.   Methods/procedure/approach: What did you actually do to get your results? (e.g. analyzed 3 novels, completed a series of 5 oil paintings, interviewed 17 students)
3.   Results/findings/product: As a result of completing the above procedure, what did you learn/invent/create?
4.   Conclusion/implications: What are the larger implications of your findings, especially for the problem/gap identified in step 1?

However, it's important to note that the weight accorded to the different components can vary by discipline. For models, try to find abstracts of research that is similar to your research.

ABSTRACT PRINCIPAL PARTS

1.   Objective
2.   Materials and Methods
3.   Results
4.   Conclusion/s

CHECKLIST: PARTS OF AN ABSTRACT [47]

Summarize the study, including the following elements in any abstract. Try to keep the first two items to no more than one sentence each.

- Purpose of the study - hypothesis, overall question, objective.
- Model organism or system and brief description of the experiment.
- Results, including specific data - if the results are quantitative in nature, report quantitative data; results of any statistical analysis shoud be reported.
- Important conclusions or questions that follow from the experiment(s).

Style

- Single paragraph, and concise.
- As a summary of work done, it is always written in past tense.
- An abstract should stand on its own, and not refer to any other part of the paper such as a figure or table.
- Focus on summarizing results - limit background information to a sentence or two, if absolutely necessary.
- What you report in an abstract must be consistent with what you reported in the paper.
- Correct spelling, clarity of sentences and phrases, and proper reporting of quantities (proper units, significant figures) are just as important in an abstract as they are anywhere else.

Despite the fact that an abstract is quite brief, it must do almost as much work as the multi-page paper that follows it. In a computer architecture paper, this means that it should in most cases include the following sections. Each section is typically a single sentence, although there is room for creativity. In particular, the parts may be merged or spread among a set of sentences. Use the following as a checklist for your next abstract [56]:

- *Motivation*: *Why do we care* about the problem and the results? If the problem isn't obviously "interesting" it might be better to put motivation first; but if your work is incremental progress on a problem that is widely recognized as important, then it is probably better to put the problem statement first to indicate which piece of the larger problem you are breaking off to work on. This section should include the importance of your work, the difficulty of the area, and the impact it might have if successful.
- *Problem statement*: What *problem* are you trying to solve? What is the *scope* of your work (a generalized approach, or for a specific

situation)? Be careful not to use too much jargon. In some cases it is appropriate to put the problem statement before the motivation, but usually this only works if most readers already understand why the problem is important.

- *Approach: How did you go about solving* or making progress on the problem? Did you use simulation, analytic models, prototype construction, or analysis of field data for an actual product? What was the *extent* of your work (did you look at one application program or a hundred programs in twenty different programming languages?) What important *variables* did you control, ignore, or measure?

- *Results: What's the answer?* Specifically, most good computer architecture papers conclude that something is so many percent faster, cheaper, smaller, or otherwise better than something else. Put the result there, in numbers. Avoid vague, hand-waving results such as "very", "small", or "significant." If you must be vague, you are only given license to do so when you can talk about orders-of-magnitude improvement. There is a tension here in that you should not provide numbers that can be easily misinterpreted, but on the other hand you don't have room for all the caveats.

- *Conclusions: What are the implications* of your answer? Is it going to change the world (unlikely), be a significant "win", be a nice hack, or simply serve as a road sign indicating that this path is a waste of time (all of the previous results are useful). Are your results *general*, potentially generalizable, or specific to a particular case?

Other Considerations in Abstract Writing [56]

An abstract must be a fully self-contained, capsule description of the paper. It can't assume (or attempt to provoke) the reader into flipping through looking for an explanation of what is meant by some vague statement. It must make sense all by itself. Some points to consider include:

- Meet the word count limitation. If your abstract runs too long, either it will be rejected or someone will take a chainsaw to it to get it down to size.

  Your purposes will be better served by doing the difficult task of cutting yourself, rather than leaving it to someone else who might be more interested in meeting size restrictions than in representing your efforts in the best possible manner. An abstract word limit of 150 to 200 words is common.

- Any major restrictions or limitations on the results should be stated, if only by using "weasel-words" such as "might", "could", "may", and "seem".

- Think of a half-dozen search phrases and keywords that people looking for your work might use. Be sure that those exact phrases appear in your abstract, so that they will turn up at the top of a search result listing.

- Usually the context of a paper is set by the publication it appears in (for example, *IEEE Computer* magazine's articles are generally about computer technology). But, if your paper appears in a somewhat un-traditional venue, be sure to include in the problem statement the domain or topic area that it is really applicable to.

- Some publications request "keywords". These have two purposes. They are used to facilitate keyword index searches, which are greatly reduced in importance now that on-line abstract text searching is commonly used.

  However, they are also used to assign papers to review committees or editors, which can be extremely important to your fate. So make sure that the keywords you pick make assigning your paper to a review category obvious (for example, if there is a list of conference topics, use your chosen topic area as one of the keyword tuples).

- Write your summary after the rest of the paper is completed. After all, how can you summarize something that is not yet written? Economy of words is important throughout any paper, but especially in an abstract.

- However, use complete sentences and do not sacrifice readability for brevity. You can keep it concise by wording sentences so that they serve more than one purpose.

  For example, "In order to learn the role of protein synthesis in early development of the sea urchin, newly fertilized embryos were pulse-labeled with tritiated leucine, to provide a time course of changes in synthetic rate, as measured by total counts per minute (cpm)." This sentence provides the overall question, methods, and type of analysis, all in one sentence. The writer can now go directly to summarizing the results [47].

How Do You Know When You Have Enough Information in Your Abstract? [55]

A simple rule-of-thumb is to imagine that you are another researcher doing a study similar to the one you are reporting.

If your Abstract was the only part of the paper you could access, would you be happy with the information presented there?

Style

The Abstract is ONLY text. Use the active voice when possible, but much of it may require passive constructions.

Write your Abstract using concise, but complete, sentences, and get to the point quickly. Use past tense. Maximum length should be 200-300 words, usually in a single paragraph.

The Abstract *should not* contain:

- lengthy background information,
- references to other literature,
- elliptical (i.e., ending with ...) or incomplete sentences,
- abbreviations or terms that may be confusing to readers,
- any sort of illustration, figure, or table, or references to them.
- Strategy

Although it is the first section of your paper, the Abstract, by definition, must be written last since it will summarize the paper.

To begin composing your Abstract, take whole sentences or key phrases from each section and put them in a sequence which summarizes the paper. Then set about revising or adding words to make it all cohesive and clear.

As you become more proficient you will most likely compose the Abstract from scratch.

Check Your Work

Once you have the completed abstract, check to make sure that the information in the abstract completely agrees with what is written in the paper. Confirm that *all* the information appearing the abstract actually appears in the body of the paper.

KEYWORDS

Conditions

Keywords may be added to enhance the title. Space is provided on the agreement form for you to suggest keywords. Also the key word will help the researchers to reach t your article by searching in internet.

Abstract

Four browse tree foliages (*Cassia fistula, Schinus molle, Chorisia speciosa* and *Eucalyptus camaldulensis*), native to the semi-arid region of north Egypt, were harvested during the dry season and evaluated for nutritional quality by determination of levels of nutrient and secondary compounds, as well as feed intake and apparent digestibility in sheep and goats. The study consisted of four experiments conducted in sequential 28-day periods that were the same in all respects, except that a different foliage was evaluated in each experiment which used six adult male Rhmani sheep (35 ± 2.3 kg body weight (BW) at the start of the study) and six crossbred goats (30 ± 1.56 kg BW). Sheep and goats were randomly divided into two groups of three and offered foliage at a level equal to 1.3 of the previous days voluntary intake of fresh matter and a commercial concentrate, with or without 10 g/animal/d of PEG, at 10 g/kg of BW to meet 0.7 of maintenance metabolizable energy requirements. Foliage crude protein (CP) content ranged from 124 (*S. molle*) and 128 (*C. speciosa*) to 185 g/kg DM (*C. fistula*). Ether extract was highest (97 g/kg) in *S. molle*. *C. fistula* had the lowest neutral detergent fiber

Abbreviations: BW, body weight; ADFom, acid detergent fiber; NDFom, neutral detergent fiber; Lignin(sa), acid detergent lignin; CP, crude protein; DM, dry matter; PEG, polyethylene glycol; TP, total phenolics; CT, condensed tannins; SAP, saponins; ALKA, alkaloids; AF, the aqueous fraction

* Corresponding author. Tel.: +20 3 5292727; fax: +20 3 5901900.
  E-mail address: asalem70@yahoo.com (A.Z.M. Salem).

252   *A.Z.M. Salem et al. / Animal Feed Science and Technology 127 (2006) 251–267*

(NDFom), acid detergent fiber (ADFom) and acid detergent lignin (lignin(sa)), while *E. camaldulensis* had the highest values. Total phenolics (TP), condensed tannins (CT), saponins (SAP), alkaloids (ALKA), the aqueous fraction (AF) of lectins, polypeptides and starch, and essential oils (EO) were lowest in *C. speciosa* (29, 21, 3, 0, 4 g/kg DM and 0.40 ml/kg DM, respectively) and highest in *E. camaldulensis* (102, 68, 15, 5, 3 g/kg DM and 15 ml/kg DM, respectively). Levels of TP, CT, SAP, ALKA and EO were highly positively intercorrelated among foliages, although AF was weakly negatively correlated to all others. Goats consumed 3.9% more foliage dry matter (DM) than sheep per kg $BW^{0.75}$, and their digestibility was about 8% higher, probably reflecting their better capacity to detoxify secondary compounds in the rumen than sheep. Levels of CT (and due to its correlations, also TP, SAP, ALKA and EO) was a strong predictor of DM intake of PEG unsupplemented foliages within both sheep and goats. PEG increased ($P<0.05$) intake of DM and its components in sheep and goats. Digestion of DM and NDFom were not affected by feeding PEG, although digestion of OM, EE and CP were higher ($P<0.05$). TP in tree foliages (and due to its correlations, also CT, SAP, ALKA and EO) was not a predictor of the proportional increase in DM with PEG feeding, which was best predicted by level of CP within foliage. Overall, *C. speciosa*, had the highest nutrient value for both sheep and goats, both without and with PEG feeding. *S. molle* and *C. fistula* were intermediate and *E. camaldulensis* had the lowest nutritive value.

Keywords: Foliage; Secondary compounds; Feed intake; Digestibility; Sheep; Goats

Example 1.

Abstract

In vitro gas production (IVGP) and dry matter degradability (IVDMD) of *Acacia saligna* leaves (ASL) from four seasons were studied under arid Egyptian conditions as a 4×3 factorial experiment (4 seasons $\times$ 3 ruminant species). Incubations were completed using rumen liquid collected immediately after slaughter from sheep, cattle and buffalo, in order to investigate differences among ruminants in their ASL fermentation capacity. Samples of ASL were collected during the last 2 months of each season, being autumn, winter, spring and summer (between the 5th and 12th week of each season). Dried samples of ASL were incubated for 24 h in each of the three buffered rumen liquors, using a syringe technique, to determine IVGP and IVDMD. The crude protein content of ASL was lower ($P<0.01$) in summer (143 g/kg DM) than autumn (171 g/kg DM), winter (177 g/kg DM) and spring (182 g/kg DM). In winter, ASL had lower neutral detergent fibre, acid detergent fibre, acid detergent lignin and cellulose than in other seasons ($P<0.05$), but there were no differences among seasons in ash and hemicellulose contents. Condensed tannin (CT, as quebracho tannin equivalent) contents of ASL were higher ($P<0.001$) in summer (113 g/kg DM) versus the other seasons, with the lowest value during winter (63 g/kg DM). Gas production after 24 h was higher ($P<0.05$) with buffalo rumen fluid, versus cattle or sheep, in all seasons except winter. IVGP with buffalo rumen fluid was not affected by season but, with cattle and sheep, IVGP was higher ($P<0.01$) in winter. IVDMD was higher in winter

Abbreviations: ADF, acid detergent fibre; ADL, acid detergent lignin; CEL, cellulose; CP, crude protein; CT, condensed tannins; DM, dry matter; GY, gas yield; HCEL, hemicellulose; IVDMD, in vitro DM degradability; IVGP, in vitro gas production; NDF, neutral detergent fibre; RGP, rate of gas production

* Corresponding author. Tel.: +203 5292727; fax: +203 5901900.

E-mail address: asalem70@yahoo.com.

0377-8401/$ – see front matter © 2005 Elsevier B.V. All rights reserved.

doi:10.1016/j.anifeedsci.2005.04.042

68   A.-F.Z.M. Salem / Animal Feed Science and Technology 123–124 (2005) 67–79

and spring, and lower in summer and autumn, within all species, and higher ($P<0.001$) values were general with buffalo versus other species. IVGP was positively ($P<0.05$) correlated with IVDMD, but there was no consistent relationship between IVGP or IVDMD and chemical composition of ASL. Rumen fluid from buffalo, cattle and sheep have different capacities to ferment *A. saligna* leaves, and differences among species were smallest in winter, when the fibre and CT contents of ASL were lower. © 2005 Elsevier B.V. All rights reserved.

Keywords: Seasonal variation; *Acacia saligna*; Condensed tannins; Gas production; Dry matter degradability; Buffalo; Cattle; Sheep

Example 2.

ARTICLE INFO

Article history:
Received 10 September 2008
Received in revised form 16 October 2009
Accepted 4 December 2009

Keywords:
Browse
Cows
Degradability
Goats
Dry season
Rainy season

ABSTRACT

Browse foliages from *Lysiloma acapulcencis, Quercus laeta* and *Pithecellobium dulce*, native to the subtropical region of southern México, were harvested during the dry season (DS) and rainy season (RS) to determine *in situ* degradability using ruminal inoculum from fistulated cows as well as goats previously adapted (AG) or not adapted (UG) to browse species fed in their daily diet. Browse leaf samples were incubated in the rumen of each group for 48 h. The crude protein (CP) content of browse was considerably higher in RS ($P<0.001$). *P. dulce* had the lowest neutral detergent fiber (NDFom) and acid detergent fiber (ADFom) in the two seasons; *L. acapulcencis* had the highest values and *Q. laeta* values were intermediate, with an overall increase in fiber fractions in DS browse foliage ($P<0.001$). The lowest *in situ* degradability values were in *L. acapulcencis* and *Q. laeta* had intermediate values during both seasons. Season of harvest (RS or DS), and ruminal inoculum (cows, UG, and AG) affected ($P<0.001$) dry matter degradability (DMD), crude protein degradability (CPD) and fiber fractions of browse. Nutrient degradabilities in all species were higher ($P<0.001$) in DS than RS. Goats previously exposed to these browse species (AG) had higher ($P<0.001$) *in situ* degradability of the browse species than cows or goats in UG fed diets without browse. Overall, goats had higher ($P<0.001$) nutrient *in situ* degradability than cows. Our results suggest higher potential of these browse species as forages for ruminants during the dry period in semi-arid regions, but goats previously exposed to diets supplemented with the browse species had a better ability to degrade them than cows or goats in UG. *P. dulce* has the highest potential as a feed protein source in small ruminants during the dry period.
© 2009 Elsevier B.V. All rights reserved.

Example 3.

Chapter 3

INTRODUCTION AND MATERIAL METHODS

INTRODUCTION SECTION [59]

The introduction to a paper is a very important section, in that it sets the expectations of the reader. The purpose of an introduction is to acquaint the reader with the rationale behind the work, with the intention of defending it. It places your work in a theoretical context, and enables the reader to understand and appreciate your objectives.

While there is no one formula for a good introduction, in general, an introduction to a formal paper of this type should accomplish the following:

- An introduction should attract the reader's attention. Magazine and newspaper articles often accomplish this with brief but interesting anecdotes, questions that pique the reader's curiosity, something of personal relevance to the reader, or other apt quotations, provocative questions, or statements. While you shouldn't feel that you have to sensationalize, neither should you assume that the reader is interested in what you have to say by default. Very often just raising the interesting issue that your thesis explores is enough to pull your reader in.

- An introduction should tell the reader explicitly what the thesis (the point of the paper) is. After having read the introduction, the reader should have no doubt about what the central point of your paper is.

- An introduction should establish the significance of your point to the reader. You should convince your audience that it should care about what you have to say, though attention to relevance and significance is part of constructing a successful thesis [60].

- An introduction can give a preview of how you are going to demonstrate your thesis. Writers often summarize in a brief list of three or so points how you are going to back up your thesis, so as to prepare the reader and improve the reader's recognition and retention of those points.

What this Handout Is About [61]

This handout will explain the functions of introductions, offer strategies for writing effective ones, help you check your drafted introductions, and provide you with examples of introductions to be avoided.

The Role of Introductions [61]

Introductions and conclusions can be the most difficult parts of papers to write. Usually when you sit down to respond to an assignment, you have at least some sense of what you want to say in the body of your paper. You might have chosen a few examples you want to use or have an idea that will help you answer the question: these sections, therefore, are not as hard to write. But these middle parts of the paper can't just come out of thin air; they need to be introduced and concluded in a way that makes sense to your reader.

Your introduction and conclusion act as bridges that transport your readers from their own lives into the "place" of your analysis. If your readers pick up your paper about education in the autobiography of Frederick Douglass, for example, they need a transition to help them leave behind the world of Chapel Hill, network television, e-mail, and the The Daily Tar Heel and to help them temporarily enter the world of nineteenth-century American slavery. By providing an introduction that helps your readers make a transition between their own world and the issues you will be writing about, you give your readers the tools they need to get into your topic and care about what you are saying. Similarly, once you've hooked your reader with the introduction and offered evidence to prove your thesis, your conclusion can provide a bridge to help your readers make the transition back to their daily lives. (See our handout on conclusions [62]).

Here are some things to watch out for in your introduction [63]:

- *An introduction is not the place to introduce background or factual information.* A common impulse is to start a paper with the story of when a person was born, or with some historical background. However, unless some brief information is necessary to understand the terms within or significance of the thesis, save the background for your next paragraph.

- *An introduction should not be too long.* An introduction should be a single paragraph, at least for the length of papers for this class. A page-long intro is usually too long -- half a page or less is good. If your opening anecdote is a long one, you don't have to finish it in the introduction -- just introduce enough of it to get the reader's attention and establish the significance of your thesis. You can finish it in the body of the paper. (In fact, such a "teaser" is a common device of newspaper feature writers).

- *Don't start your introduction with a dictionary definition.* We're not interested in how Webster's defines "Postmodernism." We are interested in YOUR take on it.

- *Don't start out with a grand generalization.* The cliche of the "pyramid form" introduction often leads to uninteresting sentences that begin with "Since the beginning of time..." or "Throughout history...". Showing the significance of your thesis does not mean that you have to demonstrate its importance in the history of art or tie it to some universal observation.

- *Your introductions should not exceed two pages* (double spaced, typed). See the examples in the writing portfolio package.

Your second paragraph will often connect the opening anecdote or statement to the rest of the paper, providing a transition from your generalized introduction to your detailed look at your first point. It is also a common technique to refer back to your opening in your conclusion, providing a satisfying closure to the paper.

Although a successful introduction will follow these general guidelines, none of them should imply a rigid formula, nor will I expect one.

Generally, a good paper introduction is fairly formulaic. If you follow a simple set of rules, you can write a very good introduction. The following outline can be varied. For example, you can use two paragraphs instead of one, or you can place more emphasis on one aspect of the intro than another. But in all cases, all of the points below need to be covered in an introduction, and in most papers, you don't need to cover anything more in an introduction.

Paragraph 1: Motivation. At a high level, what is the problem area you are working in and why is it important? It is important to set the larger context here. Why is the problem of interest and importance to the larger community?

Paragraph 2: What is the specific problem considered in this paper? This paragraph narrows down the topic area of the paper. In the first paragraph you have established general context and importance. Here you establish specific context and background.

Paragraph 3: "In this paper, we show that ...". This is the key paragraph in the intro - you summarize, in one paragraph, what are the main contributions of your paper given the context you have established in paragraphs 1 and 2. What is the general approach taken? Why are the specific results significant? This paragraph must be really really good. If you can't "sell" your work at a high level in a paragraph in the intro, then you are in trouble. As a reader or reviewer, this is the paragraph that I always look for, and read very carefully.

You should think about how to structure this one or two paragraph summary of what your paper is all about. If there are two or three main results, then you might consider itemizing them with bullets or in test (e.g., "First, ..."). If the results fall broadly into two categories, you can bring out that distinction here. For example, "Our results are both theoretical and applied in nature. (two sentences follow, one each on theory and application)".

Paragraph 4: At a high level what are the differences in what you are doing, and what others have done? Keep this at a high level, you can refer to a future section where specific details and differences will be given. But it is important for the reader to know at a high level, what is new about this work compared to other work in the area.

Paragraph 5: "The remainder of this paper is structured as follows..." Give the reader a roadmap for the rest of the paper. Avoid redundant phrasing, "In Section 2, In section 3, ... In Section 4, ... " etc. [63]

The function of the Introduction is to [64]:

- Establish the context of the work being reported. This is accomplished by discussing the relevant primary research literature [65] (with citations [66]) and summarizing our current understanding of the problem you are investigating;
- State the purpose [67] of the work in the form of the hypothesis, question, or problem you investigated; and,

- Briefly explain your rationale [68] and approach and, whenever possible, the possible outcomes your study can reveal.

Quite literally, the Introduction must answer the questions, "What was I studying? Why was it an important question? What did we know about it before I did this study? How will this study advance our knowledge?".

Writing an Introduction [69,70]

The abstract is the only text in a research paper to be written without using paragraphs in order to separate major points. Approaches vary widely, however for our studies the following approach can produce an effective introduction.

- Describe the importance (significance) of the study - why was this worth doing in the first place? Provide a broad context.
- Defend the model - why did you use this particular organism or system? What are its advantages? You might comment on its suitability from a theoretical point of view as well as indicate practical reasons for using it.
- Provide a rationale. State your specific hypothesis(es) or objective(s), and describe the reasoning that led you to select them.
- Very briefly describe the experimental design and how it accomplished the stated objectives.
- Begin your Introduction by clearly identifying the subject area of interest. Do this by using *key words* from your Title [71] in the first few sentences of the Introduction to get it focused directly on topic at the appropriate level. This insures that you get to the primary subject matter quickly without losing focus, or discussing information that is too general. For example, in the mouse behavior paper, the words *hormones* and *behavior* would likely appear within the first one or two sentences of the Introduction.
- Establish the *context* by providing a brief and balanced review of the pertinent published literature that is available on the subject. The key is to summarize (for the reader) what we knew about the specific problem *before* you did your experiments or studies. This is accomplished with a general review of the *primary research literature* (with citations [72]) but should not include very specific, lengthy

explanations that you will probably discuss in greater detail later in the Discussion [73]. The judgment of what is general or specific is difficult at first, but with practice and reading of the scientific literature you will develop e firmer sense of your audience. In the mouse behavior paper, for example, you would begin the Introduction at the level of mating behavior in general, and then quickly focus to mouse mating behaviors and then hormonal regulation of behavior. Lead the reader to your statement of purpose/hypothesis by focusing your literature review from the more general context (the big picture e.g., hormonal modulation of behaviors) to the more specific topic of interest to you (e.g., role/effects of reproductive hormones, especially estrogen, in modulating specific sexual behaviors of mice).

- What literature should you look for in your review of what we know about the problem? Focus your efforts on the *primary research journals* - the journals that publish original research articles. Although you may read some general background references (encyclopedias, textbooks, lab manuals, style manuals, etc.) to get yourself acquainted with the subject area, do not cite these, because they contain information that is considered fundamental or "common" knowledge within the discipline. Cite, instead, articles that reported specific results relevant to your study. Learn, as soon as possible, how to find the *primary literature* (research journals) and *review articles* rather than depending on reference books. The articles listed in the Literature Cited of relevant papers you find are a good starting point to move *backwards* in a line of inquiry. Most academic libraries support the Citation Index - an index which is useful for tracking a line of inquiry *forward* in time. Some of the newer search engines will actually send you alerts of new papers that cite particular articles of interest to you. *Review articles* are particularly useful because they summarize all the research done on a narrow subject area over a brief period of time (a year to a few years in most cases).

- Be sure to clearly state the purpose and /or hypothesis that you investigated. When you are first learning to write in this format it is okay, and actually preferable, to use a pat statement like, "The purpose of this study was to...." or "We investigated three possible mechanisms to explain the ... (1) blah, blah...(2) etc. It is most usual to place the statement of purpose near the end of the Introduction, often as the topic sentence of the final paragraph. It is not necessary (or even desirable) to use the words "hypothesis" or "null hypothesis",

since these are usually implicit if you clearly state your purpose and expectations.

- Provide a clear statement of the rationale for your approach to the problem studied. For example: State briefly how you approached the problem (e.g., you studied oxidative respiration pathways in isolated mitochondria of cauliflower). This will usually follow your statement of purpose in the last paragraph of the Introduction. Why did you choose this kind of experiment or experimental design? What are the scientific merits of this particular *model* system? What advantages does it confer in answering the particular question(s) you are posing? Do not discuss here the actual *techniques* or *protocols* used in your study (this will be done in the Materials and Methods [74]); your readers will be quite familiar with the usual techniques and approaches used in your field. If you are using a *novel* (new, revolutionary, and never used before) technique or methodology, the merits of the new technique/method versus the previously used methods *should be* presented in the Introduction.

Style [69]

- Use past tense except when referring to established facts. After all, the paper will be submitted after all of the work is completed.
- Organize your ideas, making one major point with each paragraph. If you make the four points listed above, you will need a minimum of four paragraphs.
- Present background information only as needed in order support a position. The reader does not want to read everything you know about a subject.
- State the hypothesis/objective precisely - do not oversimplify.
- As always, pay attention to spelling, clarity and appropriateness of sentences and phrases.

The structure of the Introduction can be thought of as an inverted triangle - the broadest part at the top representing the most general information and focusing down to the specific problem you studied. Organize the information to present the more general aspects of the topic early in the Introduction, then narrow toward the more specific topical information that provides context,

finally arriving at your statement of purpose and rationale. A good way to get on track is to sketch out the Introduction *backwards*; start with the specific purpose and then decide what is the scientific context in which you are asking the question(s) your study addresses. Once the scientific context is decided, then you'll have a good sense of what level and type of general information with which the Introduction should begin [68].

Conditions

- In this section you will descript the major problems which you would to resolve it by your research work done in this paper and some details about thesis problems.
- You will use the previous studies published in that area of your paper. At the final part of the introduction you need to add your aim/s from your study in this paper.

Principal Sections

1. Major problem/s
2. Problem/s details
3. Aim/s of resolving the problem/s

Citations in the Body of the Paper
(for More Details, Please See Chapter 5)

How to write the references within your manuscript text?

- Salem, A.Z.M., 2005 >>>>> Salem (2005).
- Salem, A.Z.M., El-Adawy, M.M., Gado, H., Khalil, M.S.M., 2007 >>>>>>>>>> Salem *et al.*, (2007).
- Salem, A.Z.M., Goher, Y.M., 2009 >>> Salem and Goher (2009).

Why Bother Writing a Good Introduction? [61]

1. You never get a second chance to make a first impression. The opening paragraph of your paper will provide your readers with their initial impressions of your argument, your writing style, and the overall quality of your work. A vague, disorganized, error-filled, off

the-wall, or boring introduction will probably create a negative impression. On the other hand, a concise, engaging, and well-written introduction will start your readers off thinking highly of you, your analytical skills, your writing, and your paper. This impression is especially important when the audience you are trying to reach (your instructor) will be grading your work.

2. Your introduction is an important road map for the rest of your paper. Your introduction conveys a lot of information to your readers. You can let them know what your topic is, why it is important, and how you plan to proceed with your discussion. It should contain a thesis that will assert your main argument. It will also, ideally, give the reader a sense of the kinds of information you will use to make that argument and the general organization of the paragraphs and pages that will follow. After reading your introduction, your readers should not have any major surprises in store when they read the main body of your paper.

3. Ideally, your introduction will make your readers want to read your paper. The introduction should capture your readers' interest, making them want to read the rest of your paper. Opening with a compelling story, a fascinating quotation, an interesting question, or a stirring example can get your readers to see why this topic matters and serve as an invitation for them to join you for an interesting intellectual conversation [61].

Strategies for Writing an Effective Introduction [61]

- Start by thinking about the question. Your entire essay will be a response to the assigned question, and your introduction is the first step toward that end. Your direct answer to the assigned question will be your thesis, and your thesis will be included in your introduction, so it is a good idea to use the question as a jumping off point. Imagine that you are assigned the following question:

- Education has long been considered a major force for American social change, righting the wrongs of our society. Drawing on The Narrative of the Life of Frederick Douglass, discuss the relationship between education and slavery in 19th-century America. Consider the following: How did white control of education reinforce slavery? How did Douglass and other enslaved African Americans view education while they endured slavery? And what role did education play in the acquisition of freedom? Most importantly, consider the degree to which education was or was not a major force for social change with regard to slavery [61].

- You will probably refer back to this question extensively as you prepare your complete essay, and the question itself can also give you some clues about how to approach the introduction. Notice that the question starts with a broad statement, that education has been considered a major force for social change, and then narrows to focus on specific questions from the book. One strategy might be to use a similar model in your own introduction —start off with a big picture sentence or two about the power of education as a force for change as a way of getting your reader interested and then focus in on the details of your argument about Douglass. Of course, a different approach could also be very successful, but looking at the way the professor set up the question can sometimes give you some ideas for how you might answer it. Keep in mind, though, that even a "big picture" opening needs to be clearly related to your topic; an opening sentence that said "Human beings, more than any other creatures on earth, are capable of learning" would be too broad. (See our handout on understanding assignments for additional information on the hidden clues in assignments) [61].

- Try writing your introduction last. You may think that you have to write your introduction first, but that isn't necessarily true, and it isn't always the most effective way to craft a good introduction. You may find that you don't know what you are going to argue at the beginning of the writing process, and only through the experience of writing your paper do you discover your main argument. It is perfectly fine to start out thinking that you want to argue a particular point, but wind up arguing something slightly or even dramatically different by the time you've written most of the paper. The writing process can be an important way to organize your ideas, think through complicated issues, refine your thoughts, and develop a sophisticated argument. However, an introduction written at the beginning of that discovery process will not necessarily reflect what you wind up with at the end. You will need to revise your paper to make sure that the introduction, all of the evidence, and the conclusion reflect the argument you intend. Sometimes it helps to write up all of your evidence first and then write the introduction—that way you can be sure that the introduction matches the body of the paper [61].

- Don't be afraid to write a tentative introduction first and then change it later. Some people find that they need to write some kind of introduction in order to get the writing process started. That's fine, but if you are one of those people, be sure to return to your initial introduction later and rewrite if necessary [61].

- Open with an attention grabber. Sometimes, especially if the topic of your paper is somewhat dry or technical, opening with something catchy can help. Consider these options:

   1. an intriguing example (for example, the mistress who initially teaches Douglass but then ceases her instruction as she learns more about slavery).

   2. a provocative quotation (Douglass writes that "education and slavery were incompatible with each other").

   3. a puzzling scenario (Frederick Douglass says of slaves that "[N]othing has been left undone to cripple their intellects, darken their minds, debase their moral nature, obliterate all traces of their relationship to mankind; and yet how wonderfully they have sustained the mighty load of a most frightful bondage, under which they have been groaning for centuries!" Douglass clearly asserts that slave owners went to great lengths to destroy the mental capacities of slaves, yet his own life story proves that these efforts could be unsuccessful).

   4. a vivid and perhaps unexpected anecdote (for example, "Learning about slavery in the American history course at Frederick Douglass High School, students studied the work slaves did, the impact of slavery on their families, and the rules that governed their lives. We didn't discuss education, however, until one student, Mary, raised her hand and asked, 'But when did they go to school?' That modern high school students could not conceive of an American childhood devoid of formal education speaks volumes about the centrality of education to American youth today and also suggests the significance of the deprivation of education in past generations").

   5. a thought-provoking question (given all of the freedoms that were denied enslaved individuals in the American South, why does Frederick Douglass focus his attentions so squarely on education and literacy?) [61].

- Pay special attention to your first sentence. Start off on the right foot with your readers by making sure that the first sentence actually says something useful and that it does so in an interesting and error-free way.

- Be straightforward and confident. Avoid statements like "In this paper, I will argue that Frederick Douglass valued education." While this sentence points toward your main argument, it isn't especially interesting. It might be more effective to say what you mean in a declarative sentence. It is much more convincing to tell us that "Frederick Douglass valued education" than to tell us that you are going to say that he did. Assert your main argument confidently. After all, you can't expect your reader to believe it if it doesn't sound like you believe it! [61].

How to Evaluate Your Introduction Draft [61]

Ask a friend to read it and then tell you what he or she expects the paper will discuss, what kinds of evidence the paper will use, and what the tone of the paper will be. If your friend is able to predict the rest of your paper accurately, you probably have a good introduction.

Five Kinds of Less Effective Introductions

1. The place holder introduction. When you don't have much to say on a given topic, it is easy to create this kind of introduction. Essentially, this kind of weaker introduction contains several sentences that are vague and don't really say much. They exist just to take up the "introduction space" in your paper. If you had something more effective to say, you would probably say it, but in the meantime this paragraph is just a place holder [61].
   - *Example:* Slavery was one of the greatest tragedies in American history. There were many different aspects of slavery. Each created different kinds of problems for enslaved people.
2. The restated question introduction. Restating the question can be an effective strategy, but it can be easy to stop at JUST restating the question instead of offering a more effective, interesting introduction to your paper. The professor or teaching assistant wrote your questions and will be reading ten to seventy essays in response to them—he or she does not need to read a whole paragraph that simply restates the question. Try to do something more interesting [61].

- *Example:* Indeed, education has long been considered a major force for American social change, righting the wrongs of our society. The Narrative of the Life of Frederick Douglass discusses the relationship between education and slavery in 19th century America, showing how white control of education reinforced slavery and how Douglass and other enslaved African Americans viewed education while they endured Moreover, the book discusses the role that education played in the acquisition of freedom. Education was a major force for social change with regard to slavery [61].

3. The Webster's Dictionary introduction. This introduction begins by giving the dictionary definition of one or more of the words in the assigned question. This introduction strategy is on the right track—if you write one of these, you may be trying to establish the important terms of the discussion, and this move builds a bridge to the reader by offering a common, agreed-upon definition for a key idea. You may also be looking for an authority that will lend credibility to your paper. However, anyone can look a word up in the dictionary and copy down what Webster says— it may be far more interesting for you (and your reader) if you develop your own definition of the term in the specific context of your class and assignment. Also recognize that the dictionary is also not a particularly authoritative work—it doesn't take into account the context of your course and doesn't offer particularly detailed information. If you feel that you must seek out an authority, try to find one that is very relevant and specific. Perhaps a quotation from a source reading might prove better? Dictionary introductions are also ineffective simply because they are so overused. Many graders will see twenty or more papers that begin in this way, greatly decreasing the dramatic impact that any one of those papers will have [61].

   - *Example:* Webster's dictionary defines slavery as "the state of being a slave," as "the practice of owning slaves," and as "a condition of hard work and subjection".

4. The "dawn of man" introduction. This kind of introduction generally makes broad, sweeping statements about the relevance of this topic since the beginning of time. It is usually very general (similar to the place holder introduction) and fails to connect to the thesis. You may write this kind of introduction when you don't have much to say—which is precisely why it is ineffective [61].

- *Example:* Since the dawn of man, slavery has been a problem in human history.

5. The book report introduction. This introduction is what you had to do for your fifth-grade book reports. It gives the name and author of the book you are writing about, tells what the book is about, and offers other basic facts about the book. You might resort to this sort of introduction when you are trying to fill space because it's a familiar, comfortable format. It is ineffective because it offers details that your reader already knows and that are irrelevant to the thesis [61].

A Few General Tips [77]

- Don't spend a lot of time into the introduction telling the reader about what you don't do in the paper. Be clear about what you do, but don't dwell here on what you don't do.
- Does each paragraph have a theme sentence that sets the stage for the entire paragraph? Are the sentences and topics in the paragraph all related to each other?
- Do all of your tenses match up in a paragraph?

Examples

L.M. Camacho et al. / Animal Feed Science and Technology 155 (2010) 206–212   207

1. Introduction

The use of browse species as green forage for ruminants is becoming increasingly important in many parts of the tropics, including México. In free-ranging livestock-production systems, browse species are an important supplement to dry season forage shortages, improving both the quantity and quality of pasture. Trees and shrubs are perennials that allow provision of permanent fodder *versus* herbaceous species which decrease rapidly in quantity and quality after rains. Regular availability of forage from trees and shrubs depends on the diversity of species and their phenological variation in time and space (Grouzis and Sicot, 1980), but they have potential to alleviate feed shortages and nutritional deficiencies during the dry season on smallholder farms. The high quality of some browse in crude protein (CP) content, as well as minerals such as calcium and phosphorus (Paterson et al., 1998), is well appreciated. Tree and shrub leaves can be an important component of small ruminant diets (Papachristou and Nastis, 1996; Salem et al., 2006), and they are important in the nutrition of grazing animals in areas where few, or no, alternative feeds are available (Meuret et al., 1990). However many browse species have secondary compounds that can deter invasion and consumption of their leaves by microbes, insects and herbivorous animals. Tannins are an important class of compounds that can decrease degradability of browse fodders (Salem et al., 2006), but use of tree and shrub leaves by herbivores may be restricted by negative effects on digestion and intake of their generally high levels of several other secondary compounds (Salem, 2005; Salem et al., 2006, 2007).

Goats are effective browsers, that have the ability to utilize woody species and low-quality forages better than cattle and sheep, and can adapt to harsh environments (Silanikove, 2000; Salem et al., 2004). Extensive shrublands of evergreens and small trees, known as garrigue or maquis, that are often high in tannins and other secondary compounds are the basic components of diets of goats in the Mediterranean area (Salem et al., 2006, 2007). Previous studies suggest that progressive adaptation to tannins can be induced in any herbivore species in response to regular feeding of tanniniferous feeds (Pell et al., 2000). Animals adapted to tannins in their diet exhibit changes in rumen microbial populations, and tannin-resistant, or tolerant, bacteria can be isolated particularly from the rumen of animals previously exposed to tanniniferous feeds (Brooker et al., 2000; Odenyo et al., 2003). In México, there is limited information on the nutritive value of tree shrubs fed to livestock (Ramirez et al., 2000; Cerrillo and Juárez, 2004). Our aim was thus to investigate impacts of growing season on ruminal *in situ* degradability of some tree foliages using rumen fluid from goats (adapted or unadapted to eating tree foliage) and cows under the southern subtropical conditions in México.

Example 1.

1. Introduction

A major cause of low productivity of livestock in tropical regions, such as Egypt, is inadequate amounts, and poor nutritional quality, of many locally available feeds. Browse fodder is a potentially inexpensive locally produced protein supplement for ruminants, particularly during the critical periods of the year when the quantity and quality of herbage is limited. However, most tropical browse species contain substantial amounts of phenolic compounds, mainly tannins (Makkar and Becker, 1998; Salem, 2005) as well as other secondary compounds (Salem et al., 2004b). This can reduce their nutritional value, as most tannins bind to feed proteins thereby making them unavailable to ruminal microorganisms. Thus, the use of high tannin browse species as supplements to crop residue-based diets may not increase the productivity of animals, as ruminally available N frequently limits ruminal microbial growth and subsequent degradation of structural carbohydrates.

However, several fodder shrubs and trees have been shown to be able to partially or totally replace concentrate feeds without decreasing digestion or growth of sheep and goats. For example, Ondiek et al. (2000) concluded that *Leucaena leucocephala* and *Gliricidia sepium* foliage could contribute N in diet supplements without detrimental effects on production of dairy goats. Liu et al. (2001) showed that mulberry (*Morus alba*) leaves could be used as a protein supplement in an ammoniated rice straw diet to fully substitute for rapeseed meal.

Goats are effective browsers, have the ability to utilize woody species and low-quality forages better than cattle and sheep, and can adapt to harsh environments (Tisserand et al., 1991; Silanikove, 2000a, 2000b; Salem et al., 2004a). Extensive shrub-lands of evergreens

and small trees, known as garrigue or maquis, that are often high in tannins and other secondary compounds are the basic component of diets of goats in the Mediterranean area.

Attempts have been made to deactivate tannins, and other secondary compounds, in temperate and tropical forages. These attempts include use of polyethylene glycol (PEG), a synthetic polymer for which tannins have a greater binding affinity than proteins (Makkar, 2003a). Therefore, PEG releases forage proteins from tannin–protein complexes and improves their nutritional value. Degen et al. (1998, 2000) used *Acacia saligna*, a tannin-rich leguminous shrub species, and suggested that effects of PEG may persist for up to 14 days in sheep and goats after PEG feeding is terminated.

This study was designed to determine the nutritive value of four browse tree species in terms of nutrient and secondary compounds, and to assess the capability of PEG added to the diet to mitigate adverse effects of secondary compounds on feed intake and nutrient digestibility in sheep and goats.

Example 2.

68   *A.-F.Z.M. Salem / Animal Feed Science and Technology 123–124 (2005) 67–79*

and spring, and lower in summer and autumn, within all species, and higher ($P<0.001$) values were general with buffalo versus other species. IVGP was positively ($P<0.05$) correlated with IVDMD, but there was no consistent relationship between IVGP or IVDMD and chemical composition of ASL. Rumen fluid from buffalo, cattle and sheep have different capacities to ferment *A. saligna* leaves, and differences among species were smallest in winter, when the fibre and CT contents of ASL were lower.

Keywords: Seasonal variation; *Acacia saligna*; Condensed tannins; Gas production; Dry matter degradability; Buffalo; Cattle; Sheep

1. Introduction

Browse species play a major role as feeds for ruminants in arid and semi-arid regions, particularly during the dry season when poor quality forage and crop residues are common (Ahn et al., 1989; Kibon and Ørskov, 1993). During these dry periods, forage trees remain green and maintain a relatively high crude protein (CP) content (D'Mello, 1992), and their foliage is commonly used as a protein and energy supplement to ruminants fed low quality forages (Reed et al., 1990). However, legume trees and shrubs contain a wider range of secondary compounds than conventional fodders (D'Mello, 1992). Thus, although they may contain adequate concentrations of nutrients, the presence of these compounds could present constraints to their use as feed supplements (Dzowela et al., 1987).

Many browse species are associated with deleterious effects on livestock performance either due to toxic and/or secondary compounds that can reduce feed intake and nutrient utilization. Salem et al. (2004) detected phenolic compounds, saponins, alkaloids and lectins, which can be highly toxic to ruminal and intestinal bacteria, in *Acacia saligna* leaves (ASL). However the primary secondary compound in *Acacia* species, and many other browse species, appears to be condensed tannins (CT), which are widely distributed in leaves of trees and shrubs (D'Mello, 1992), but occur in leaves and stems of only a small number of specialized non-woody forage legume plants (Barry, 1989).

Little information is available on effects of seasonal variation on the nutritive value of *A. saligna* leaves to different ruminant species. The objective was to investigate impacts of season on chemical composition, in vitro gas production and dry matter (DM) degradability of *A. saligna* leaves using rumen fluid from three ruminant species under the arid conditions of north Egypt.

Example 3.

MATERIAL AND METHODS SECTION

There is no specific page limit, but a key concept is to keep this section as concise as you possibly can. People will want to read this material selectively. The reader may only be interested in one formula or part of a procedure.

Materials and methods may be reported under separate subheadings within this section or can be incorporated together.

This should be the easiest section to write, but many students misunderstand the purpose. The objective is to document all specialized materials and general procedures, so that another individual may use some or all of the methods in another study or judge the scientific merit of your work. It is not to be a step by step description of everything you did, nor is a methods section a set of instructions. In particular, it is not supposed to tell a story. By the way, your notebook should contain all of the information that you need for this section [69].

In this section you explain *clearly* how you carried out your study in the following *general* structure and organization (details follow below) [70]:

- The organism(s) studied [78] (plant, animal, human, etc.) and their pre-experiment handling and care, and when and where the study was carried out (*only* if location and time are important factors); note that the term "subject" is used ONLY for human studies.
- If a field study, a description of the study site [79], including the significant physical and biological features, and precise location (latitude and longitude, map, etc).
- The experimental OR sampling design [80] (i.e., how the experiment or study was structured. For example, controls, treatments, the variable(s) measured, how many samples were collected, replication, etc.).
- The protocol for collecting data [81], i.e., how the experimental procedures were carried out.
- How the data were analyzed [82] (qualitative analyses and/or statistical procedures used).

Organize your presentation so your reader will understand the logical flow of the experiment(s); *subheadings* work well for this purpose. Each experiment or procedure should be presented as a unit, even if it was broken up over time. The experimental design and procedure are sometimes most efficiently presented as an integrated unit, because otherwise it would be difficult to split them up. In general, provide enough quantitative detail [83] (how much, how long, when, etc.) about your experimental protocol such that other scientists could reproduce your experiments. You should also indicate the statistical procedures [84] used to analyze your results, including the probability level at which you determined significance (usually at 0.05 probability).

WRITING A MATERIALS AND METHODS SECTION [69]

Materials

- Describe materials separately only if the study is so complicated that it saves space this way.
- Include specialized chemicals, biological materials, and any equipment or supplies that are not commonly found in laboratories.
- Do not include commonly found supplies such as test tubes, pipette tips, beakers, etc., or standard lab equipment such as centrifuges, spectrophotometers, pipettors, etc.
- If use of a specific type of equipment, a specific enzyme, or a culture from a particular supplier is critical to the success of the experiment, then it and the source should be singled out, otherwise no.
- Materials may be reported in a separate paragraph or else they may be identified along with your procedures.
- In biosciences we frequently work with solutions - refer to them by name and describe completely, including concentrations of all reagents, and pH of aqueous solutions, solvent if non-aqueous [69].

Methods

- See the examples in the writing portfolio package.
- Report the methodology (not details of each procedure that employed the same methodology).
- Describe the methodology completely, including such specifics as temperatures, incubation times, etc.
- To be concise, present methods under headings devoted to specific procedures or groups of procedures.
- Generalize - report how procedures were done, not how they were specifically performed on a particular day. For example, report "samples were diluted to a final concentration of 2 mg/ml protein;" don't report that "135 microliters of sample one was diluted with 330

microliters of buffer to make the protein concentration 2 mg/ml."
Always think about what would be relevant to an investigator at
another institution, working on his/her own project.

- If well documented procedures were used, report the procedure by
  name, perhaps with reference, and that's all. For example, the
  Bradford assay is well known. You need not report the procedure in
  full - just that you used a Bradford assay to estimate protein
  concentration, and identify what you used as a standard. The same is
  true for the SDS-PAGE method, and many other well known
  procedures in biology and biochemistry [69].

Style

- It is awkward or impossible to use active voice when documenting
  methods without using first person, which would focus the reader's
  attention on the investigator rather than the work. Therefore when
  writing up the methods most authors use third person passive voice.
- Use normal prose in this and in every other section of the paper –
  avoid informal lists, and use complete sentences.
- The style in this section should read as if you were verbally describing
  the conduct of the experiment. You may use the active voice to a
  certain extent, although this section requires more use of third person,
  passive constructions than others. Avoid use of the first person in this
  section. Remember to use the *past tense* throughout - the work being
  reported is done, and was performed in the past, not the future. The
  Methods section *is not* a step-by-step, directive, protocol as you might
  see in your lab manual [70].

Conditions

- All the material and methods used in this research work shout be
  descriping in details in this section of the paper.
- The details of the material and Methods section should be give any
  one to reaped this experiment at his location.
- Divided the Materials and Methods section to a different sub-sections
  will be more useful for the researchers when red it.

- References of the reported assays or methodology which used in this experiment/s should be added clearly.
- Describe the organism(s) used in the study. This includes giving the *source* (supplier or *where* and *how* collected), *size (weight, length, etc)*, *how they were handled* before the experiment, what they were fed, etc. In genetics studies include the strains or genetic stocks used. For some studies, age is important.
- Describe the site where your field study was conducted. The description must include both *physical* and *biological* characteristics of the site pertinent to the study aims. Include the date(s) of the study (e.g., 10-15 April 1994) and the exact location of the study area. Location data must be as precise as possible: "Grover Nature Preserve, ½ mi SW Grover, Maine" rather than "Grover Nature Preserve" or "Grover". When possible, give the actual latitude and longitude position of the site (the WWW has sites which provide this service). It is most often a good idea to include a map (labeled as a Figure) showing the location in relation to some larger more recognizable geographic area. Someone else should be able to go to the exact location of your study if they want to repeat or check your work, or just visit your study area [70].

NOTE: For laboratory studies you need *not* report the date and location of the study *UNLESS* it is relevant. Most often it is *not*. If you have performed experiments at a particular location or lab because it is the only place to do it, then you should note that in your methods and identify the lab or facility [70].

- Describe your experimental design clearly. Be sure to include the *hypotheses* you tested, *controls*, *treatments*, *variables* measured, how many *replicates* you had, what you actually *measured*, what form the *data* take, etc. Always identify treatments by the variable or treatment name, NOT by an ambiguous, generic name or number (e.g., use "2.5% NaCl" rather than "test 1".) When your paper includes more than one experiment, use subheadings [85] to help organize your presentation by experiment. A general experimental design worksheet [86] is available to help plan your experiments in the core courses.
- Describe the protocol for your study in sufficient detail that other scientists could repeat your work to verify your findings. Foremost in your description should be the "quantitative" aspects of your study - the masses, volumes, incubation times, concentrations, etc., that

another scientist needs in order to duplicate your experiment. When using standard lab or field methods and instrumentation, it is not always necessary to explain the procedures (e.g., serial dilution) or equipment used (e.g., autopipetter) since other scientists will likely be familiar with them already. You may want to identify certain types of equipment by brand or category (e.g., ultracentrifuge vs. prep centrifuge) [86].

It is appropriate to give the source for reagents used parenthetically, e.g., "....poly-l-Lysine (Sigma #1309)". When using a method described in another published source, you can save time and words by referring to it and providing the relevant citation [87] to the source. Always make sure to describe any modifications you have made of a standard or published method.

- Describe how the data were summarized and analyzed. Here you will indicate what types of data summaries and analyses were employed to answer each of the questions or hypotheses tested.

The information should include [87]*:*

1. How the data were summarized (Means, percent, etc) and how you are reporting measures of variability (SD, SEM, etc).
2. This lets you avoid having to repeatedly indicate you are using mean $\pm$ SD.
3. Data transformation (e.g., to normalize or equalize variances).
4. Statistical tests used with reference to the particular questions they address, e.g.

"A Paired t-test was used to compare mean flight duration before and after applying stabilizers to the glider's wings."

"One way ANOVA was used to compare mean weight gain in weight-matched calves fed the three different rations."

5. Any other numerical or graphical techniques used to analyze the data.

Principal Parts

1. Experimental location and period (the location and the period of carry out the experiment)

2. Experimental conditions and procedures: animals, samples, management.......)
3. Analytical methods
4. Calculations and/or Statistical analysis

What to Avoid

- Materials and methods are not a set of instructions.
- Omit all explanatory information and background - save it for the discussion.
- Omit information that is irrelevant to a third party, such as what color ice bucket you used, or which individual logged in the data.

Examples

2. Materials and methods

2.1. Area of sample collection

Tree fodder species were collected from the South of Estado de México (Tejupilco) and the related metabolic work and laboratory analyses were completed at the Centro Universitario UAEM Temascaltepec located in the municipality of Temascaltepec de González Estado de México. Geographically, this is located at 19°02′04″ north latitude and 100°02′14″ west longitude at an elevation of 1720 masl. The climate is moderately humid with an average temperature of 15–18 °C and annual rainfall of 950–1000 mm (García, 1987).

2.2. Browse species

We sampled a mixture of young and mature leaves from three browse species – Tepehuaje (*Lysiloma acapulcencis*), Encino prieto (*Quercus laeta*) and Pinzan (*Pithecellobium dulce*) – that contain different levels of CT (high, medium, and low) from several locations in the South of Estado de México. Plant samples (~5 kg) were randomly collected up to a height of 1.5 m from at least 7 trees for each browse species during the rainy (i.e., August/September, 2006) and dry (April/May, 2007) seasons. Samples of each species were pooled to three samples and air dried in the shade to minimize changes in tannins content and activity (Makkar and Singh, 1991; Yousef and Rouzbehan, 2008; Robinson et al., 2006).

2.3. Analytical methods

Fresh samples were dried at 45 °C for 48 h for moisture determination and ground in a Willey-mill to pass a 1 mm screen. Ground samples were analyzed for dry matter (DM) by drying at 105 °C for 24 h in a forced air oven. Ash content was measured after igniting samples in a muffle furnace at 550 °C for 4 h. The CP was determined by the Kjeldahl method (AOAC, 1990; ID 954.01). Neutral detergent fiber (NDFom) and acid detergent fiber (ADFom) were determined by the methods of Van Soest et al. (1991) with NDFom assayed without use of an alpha amylase, but with sodium sulfite. Both NDFom and ADFom are expressed without residual ash. Total condensed tannins (TCT) were assayed using the butanol-HCL method (Terrill et al., 1992), modified by López et al. (2004), as internal standards using *L. acapulsencis*. Analyses of the free, protein-bound and fiber-bound CT were conducted, according to the method of Porter et al. (1986). The purification was performed with Sephadex LH-20 as described by Asquith and Butler (1985) with modifications by Hagerman (1991). Tannin results were the starting point for categorizing the species in three types: high (*L. acapulcencis*), medium (*Q. laeta*) and low (*P. dulce*) tannin concentrations (Table 1).

Example 1. (to be continued).

Table 1
Chemical composition and condensed tannins (g/kg DM) of the leaves of three species of browse tree during the rainy and dry seasons

Season (S)	Rainy			Dry			Sed	P value		
Browse species (B)	L. acapulcencis	Q. laeta	P. dulce	L. acapulcencis	Q. laeta	P. dulce		S	B	S×B
OM	945.9[b]	950.4[a]	909.5[d]	941.5[c]	905.6[e]	862.1[f]	7.98	<0.001	<0.001	<0.001
CP	177.0[c]	94.1[e]	261.5[a]	110.6[d]	84.7[f]	187.8[b]	9.21	<0.001	<0.001	<0.001
NDFom	607.3[a]	584.1[ab]	495.8[c]	545.0[b]	408.3[d]	357.3[e]	2.06	<0.001	<0.001	<0.001
ADFom	500.8[a]	411.8[b]	365.7[c]	478.6[a]	240.8[d]	274.7[d]	2.31	<0.001	<0.001	<0.001
Free-CT	116.3[a]	64.2[ad]	36.6[d]	101.6[ab]	80.2[bc]	68.3[cd]	6.71	0.077	<0.001	0.016
PCT	67.8[a]	23.0[c]	21.8[c]	55.8[b]	26.3[c]	21.1[c]	4.57	0.067	<0.001	0.005
FCT	3.7[b]	2.7[c]	4.1[ab]	2.8[c]	2.5[c]	4.7[a]	0.21	0.190	<0.001	0.003
TCT	187.8[a]	89.9[bc]	62.6[c]	160.2	109.0[b]	94.1[bc]	10.77	0.229	<0.001	0.004

Means with different superscripts within a row differ (P<0.05) between season of harvest of browse species. OM: organic matter, CP: crude protein, NDFom: neutral detergent fiber, ADFom: acid detergent fiber, Free-CT: free condensed tannins; PCT: protein-bound condensed tannins; FCT: fiber-bound condensed tannins; TCT: total condensed tannins, Sed: standard error of the difference.

2.4. Animals and diets

Two brown Swiss American cows (530 ± 5 kg) and 4 male Criollo×Nubia goats (34 ± 4 kg body weight) were used for sample incubation. Animals were fitted with permanent ruminal cannula about 150 days before the ruminal incubations. The 2 cows and 2 goats (unadapted goats; UG) were fed forage:concentrate (80:20; DM basis) diets. The forage contained a mixture of alfalfa hay (400 g/kg), corn silage (400 g/kg) and corn straw (200 g/kg) with a concentrate mixture (220 g/kg CP), containing ground sorghum (380 g/kg), corn (380 g/kg), soybean (120 g/kg), molasses (80 g/kg), urea (20 g/kg) and minerals (20 g/kg). The other 2 goats were fed the same concentrate mixture offered to the cows and UG, but the forage proportion was alfalfa hay (300 g/kg) and browse species (700 g/kg) composed of 128 g/kg P. dulce, 198 g/kg Quercus sp., 261 g/kg Q. laeta, 413 g/kg L. acapulcencis. The AG animals were fed this diet for 100 days before sample incubation. All animal groups were fed twice daily at 07:00 and 16:00 h. All animals had free access to vitamin–mineral mixture and clean water.

2.5. In situ degradability

In situ degradability was measured by the method of Ørskov et al. (1980) with nylon bags (5 cm×10 cm) with a pore size of 35 μm diameter. Samples of the three browse species with different contents (high, medium, and low) of CT, collected during the rainy and dry seasons, were ground to pass a 1 mm screen in a Wiley mill. Samples, 2.5 g DM/bag, were incubated in the rumen of each fistulated animal for 48 h. Three bags, of the same browse species, were introduced into the rumen of each animal species (cows, UG, and AG) before the morning feeding. The incubation was repeated with the same fistulated animal. After removal of all bags simultaneously from the rumen, bags were washed with tap water until the water was clear. They were then dried in a forced air oven at 65 °C and weighed to determine DM loss. The N and fiber fractions (NDFom and ADFom) were determined in residues to calculate the degradability.

2.6. Statistical model and analysis

Data for the chemical assays were analyzed using the general linear model (GLM) procedure in SAS (2002) for a completely randomized design with 2 seasons (rainy and dry)×3 browse species in a factorial arrangement with 3 repetitions (pooled samples) (Steel and Torrie, 1980). Means were tested using a least square means test (LSMEANS) with the statistical model:

$$Y_{ik} = \mu + S_j + B_k + S_j \times B_k + E_{jk}$$

where Y_{ik} represents response variables (chemical composition) for the two seasons (j) for each of the three browse species (k); μ – general mean; S_j – effect of j-season; B_k – effect of k-browse species; $S_j \times B_k$ – interaction of the j season with k browse species; E_{jk} – the error term – NI ($0, \sigma^2$).

Data for in situ degradability were analyzed using a randomized complete block design with 2 seasons (rainy and dry)×3 sources of inoculum (cows, UG, and AG)×3 browse species in factorial arrangement with 3 repetitions (Steel and Torrie, 1980). The mixed model was:

$$Y_{jkl} = \mu + S_j + TI_k + Sp_l + \beta_n + S_j \times TI_k \times Sp_l + E_{jkl}$$

where Y_{jkl} represents response variables (degradability of DM, CP, NDF and ADF) for the same season (j), source of ruminal inoculum (k), and browse species (l); μ – general mean; S_j – effect of j season; TI_k – effect of k-type of ruminal inoculum; Sp_l – effect of l browse species; β_n – effect of n-block (repeated incubation); $S_j \times TI_k \times Sp_l$ – interaction of the j season with k type of ruminal inoculum and l-browse species; E_{jkl} – the error term – NI ($0, \sigma^2$).

Differences among means with P<0.05, determined using a least square means test (LSMEANS), were accepted as representing statistically significant differences (Steel and Torrie, 1980).

Example 1.

2. Materials and methods

2.1. Collection of A. saligna leaves

Leaves were collected from the experimental station of the Faculty of Agriculture (Alexandria University, Alexandria, Egypt) over all seasons, being autumn (from September to November), winter (from December to February), spring (from March to May) and summer (from June to August) of 2003. Leaves were collected each week for 8 weeks

starting from the 5th week and ending in the 12th week of each season. A. saligna leaves were randomly and manually harvested from different parts of both young and mature leaves from different trees within and around the experimental station. On each week, a representative sample was collected from the same site (i.e., three samples each week). As ASL was collected in the last 8 weeks of each season, the total number of leaf samples was 32 (8 weeks × 4 seasons). Weekly samples were mixed, dried at 40 °C and stored. The DM content of each week's samples was determined in triplicate by placing samples in an oven at 40 °C to constant weight. Dried samples were ground in a hammer mill to pass a 1 mm sieve and stored in plastic bags for subsequent determination of chemical components, CT, and in vitro characterisation using rumen fluid from buffalo, cattle and sheep.

2.2. Chemical composition and condensed tannins

Procedures described by AOAC (1980) were used to determine ash and Kjeldahl N. Neutral detergent fiber (NDF), acid detergent fiber (ADF) and acid detergent lignin (ADL) were determined according to methods of Goering and Van Soest (1970). Cellulose (CEL) and hemicellulose (HCEL) contents were calculated from the difference between ADF and ADL and between NDF and ADF, respectively.

The CT were determined by Porter et al. (1986) with the modification of Makkar (2000) using butanol/HCl. Butanol/HCl (95:5, v/v) and ferric ammonium sulphate (20 g/l 2 M HCl) were used as reagents, and a solution of purified quebracho tannin (1 mg/ml aqueous acetone, 700 ml/l) was the standard. Absorbance was measured against a blank at 550 nm.

2.3. In vitro gas production (IVGP) and in vitro dry matter degradability (IVDMD)

The IVGP was determined according to Menke et al. (1979) with the modification of Salem et al. (2000). Two hundred milligrams of each sample (in triplicate) was placed in a 60 ml syringe. The piston of each syringe was lubricated with vaseline to prevent inflow of water to the syringe during incubation. Rumen fluid was collected from the rumen of the three ruminant species, that were all fed a restricted amount (about 15 g/kg of live weight) of a commercial concentrate mixture (120–140 g/kg crude protein) and wheat straw ad libitum. Immediately after slaughter, which occurred on different days, of four adult female or male animals (Egyptian buffaloes about 400–450 kg; hybrid cattle (Friesian × Egyptian cattle) about 350–400 kg, and Barki sheep about 40–45 kg) selected on the basis of their live weights and ages to minimize variation in rumen inoculum, samples of fresh digesta were collected from the rumen of each animal. All 32 ASL samples were incubated with rumen fluid from each species in four runs per species, and mixed rumen fluid from the four animals was used in each run. The samples of ASL leaves were incubated in triplicate with each species rumen fluid and repeated in four separate runs. Four blank samples were included per run. The total number of animals used in each ruminant species was 16 (4 runs × 4 animals/run) and incubations were completed during June, July and August of 2004.

In each run, rumen digesta was squeezed through four layers of cheesecloth to ensure liquor contained microbial populations from both the liquid and solid phases. Rumen liquor of each ruminant species was homogenized and kept at approximately 39 °C in a water bath,

Example 2. (to be continued).

flushed with CO_2 before use, and diluted (1.4 v:v) with the culture medium of Makkar et al. (1995), and FAO/IAEA (2000), containing bicarbonate buffer, macro-mineral, micro-mineral, resazurine and reducing solution. Buffered rumen fluid (25 ml) was pipetted into each syringe and syringes were immediately placed in a water bath at 39 °C. Gas volumes were recorded at 2, 4, 6, 10, 12 and 24 h of incubation.

At the end of the incubation (i.e., 24 h), contents of each syringe were transferred to centrifuge tubes and centrifuged at 20,000 × g for 20 min at 4 °C. The residual pellet was lyophilized in the tubes overnight. The residual moisture, if any, was removed by drying the tubes overnight at 60 °C, and then tubes were weighed and IVDMD calculated from differences between initial and residue weights, minus blank tubes.

2.4. Calculations and statistical analysis

Total gas production (IVGP) and IVDMD at 24 h were determined, and rate of gas production at 4, 6 and 11 h (RGP) was calculated from recorded volumes of gas produced before and after these times. For example, RGP at 4 h was calculated as:

$$RGP_{4h}\ (ml/g\ DM/h)$$
$$= \frac{(volume\ of\ gas\ produced\ at\ 6\ h - volume\ of\ gas\ produced\ at\ 2\ h)}{4 \times sample\ weight\ (g)}$$

Gas yields (GY_{24h}) were calculated as the volume of gas produced after 24 h of incubation divided by the amount of substrate apparently degraded.

IVGP, RGP, GY and IVDMD were analysed as a 4 × 3 factorial experiment (4 seasons × 3 ruminant species) using the general linear model of SAS (1999) with methods of Steel and Torrie (1980). Differences among seasons, species and the season × species interaction used Duncan's multiple-range test (Duncan, 1955).

Pearson correlation coefficients between IVGP, RGP, GY and IVDMD of the ruminant species in the different seasons were estimated using SAS (1999) and the correlation between IVGP, GY, IVDMD and the CT content of the ASL leaves was also estimated for each ruminant species in each season.

Example 2.

2. Materials and methods

The study was completed at the experimental station of the Faculty of Agriculture of Alexandria University in northern Egypt during May–August 2004.

2.1. Tree foliage species

Consumable parts (*i.e.*, leaves and twigs of about 1 year of age) of each foliage species used (*i.e.*, *Cassia fistula*; *Schinus molle*; *Chorisia speciosa*; *Eucalyptus camaldulensis*) were randomly harvested, by hand plucking from 8 to 10 trees of each species, every second day.

2.2. Animals, management and feeding

This study consisted of four experiments completed in sequential 28 day periods that were the same in all respects, except that a different tree foliage was evaluated in each experiment which used six adult male Rahmani sheeps and six crossbred goats weighing 35 ± 2.3 and 30 ± 1.56 kg body weight (BW), respectively, at the start of the study.

Sheep and goats were randomly divided into two groups of three to create the two experimental groups. All were offered foliage at a level equal to 1.3 of the previous days voluntary intake of fresh matter, and a commercial concentrate (with or without 10 g of PEG/animal/d; MW 4000, Analytical grade, Sigma®–Aldrich, El-Safua Co., Alexandria, Egypt) at 10 g/kg of BW to meet 0.7 of their calculated maintenance metabolizable energy (ME) requirements (NRC, 1985). The concentrate used was formulated to contain undecorticated cotton seed meal (300 g/kg), ground yellow corn (355 g/kg), wheat bran (300 g/kg), limestone (30 g/kg), salt (10 g/kg) and 5 g/kg of a trace mineral/vitamin premix (all values/kg of DM: Vitamin A, 2,000,000 IU; Vitamin D_3, 150,000 IU; Vitamin K, 0.33 mg; Vitamin B_1, 0.33 g; Vitamin B_2, 1.0 g; Vitamin B_6, 0.33 g; Vitamin B_{12}, 1.7 mg; pantathenic acid, 3.33 g; biotin, 33.0 mg; Folic acid, 0.83 g; choline chloride, 200 mg; Zn, 11.7 g; Mn, 5.0 g; Fe, 12.5 g; Mg, 66.7 mg;

Se, 16.6 mg; Co, 1.33 mg; Cu, 0.5 g; I, 16.6 mg; antioxidant, 10.0 g). The concentrate was fed at 9.00 h and animals were fed the foliage 10.00 h and allowed access to it until 2 h before the next feeding of concentrate, at which time uneaten foliage was removed and weighed. All offered concentrate was consumed by all sheep and goats within 60 min of offer on all occasions, and so orts were assumed to be foliage.

Sheep and goats were housed in individual pens during the adaptation period (*i.e.*, the first 15 days of each experiment) to the dietary treatments and had free access to clean water.

2.3. Metabolism trial (feed intake and apparent digestibility determinations)

During each experiment, after the 15 day adaptation to dietary treatments, a digestion study of 10 days duration, involving quantitative collection of feeds, refusals and faeces was conducted to determine the apparent digestibility of the diets. Animals were acclimatized to the metabolism cages for 3 days after the 15 day adaptation period and prior to the 10 day collection period. Faeces voided during each successive 24 h period were collected and weighed. Representative samples of foliage, concentrate, refusals and faeces were collected daily and dried at 105 °C to determine daily intake of DM for each animal. Other representative samples of each material, by animal for refusals and faeces, were collected daily over the 10 day collection period, bulked, mixed, sub-sampled and ground to pass a 1 mm sieve for subsequent laboratory analysis.

2.4. Analytical methods

Ground samples of feeds, refusals and frozen were analyzed for dry matter (DM) by drying samples at 105 °C for 24 h in forced air oven. Ash content was measured after igniting samples in a muffle furnace at 550 °C for 4 h. The crude protein (CP) was determined by Kjeldahl method (AOAC, 1990; ID 954.01). Ether extract (EE) was determined by Soxhlet method (AOAC, 1990; ID 920.39). Neutral detergent fiber (NDFom), acid detergent fiber (ADFom) and acid detergent lignin (lignin(sa)) were determined by methods of Van Soest et al. (1991). NDFom was assayed without the use of an alpha amylase but with use of sodium sulfite. Both NDFom and ADFom are expressed without residual ash.

Samples of each tree foliage were dried at 40 °C for 72 h and ground to pass a 1 mm sieve. All samples were thoroughly mixed and sub-sampled into four representative bulk samples of each foliage for further analysis of secondary compounds.

Approximately 200 mg (DM) of ground samples of each foliage were extracted in 10 ml of aqueous acetone (7:3 v/v) in a water bath maintained at 39–40 °C for 90 min (Makkar, 2000). Total extractable phenolics (TP) were assayed by Folin-Ciocalteu-reagent 2N (Sigma®–Aldrich, El-Safua Co., Alexandria, Egypt) based on known concentrations of tannic acid as the calibration curve (Sigma®–Aldrich) according to Makkar and Becker (1993). Condensed tannins (CT) were determined according to Porter et al. (1986) with the modification of Makkar (2000, 2003b) using butanol/HCl (95:5 v/v) and ferric ammonium sulfate (20 g/l 2 M HCl) as reagents, and a solution of purified quebracho tannin (1 mg/ml aqueous acetone, 700 ml/l) as the standard. Absorbance was measured against a blank at 550 nm.

A.Z.M. Salem et al. / Animal Feed Science and Technology 127 (2006) 251–267   255

Saponins (SAP) were extracted and isolated according to Ahmad et al. (1990), wherein dried samples are extracted with methanol several times. The combined methanol extract was evaporated and partitioned between ethanol acetate and H_2O. For the alkaloid (ALKA) extract, dried samples were first extracted with ethanol and then dissolved in dilute HCl. This solution was filtered and extracted with petroleum ether to remove fat (Arambewela and Ranatunge, 1991).

The aqueous fraction (AF) of lectins, polypeptides and starch (see review of Cowan, 1999) was determined according to Hussein et al. (1999) using fractionation by column chromatography of extracted samples by saturating the extract with distilled H_2O and 500 g/l methanol. For essential oil (EO) analysis, fresh leaves of tree foliage were cut into small pieces (0.2–0.4 cm length) with a small chopper and steam distilled. The distillate was then extracted with petroleum ether, and the resulting extract was dried on anhydrous sodium sulfate. Petroleum ether was removed carefully and EO was obtained as the liquid.

2.5. Statistical analysis

Tree foliage nutrient and secondary compound contents were statistically analyzed using the 'PROC GLM' procedure of SAS (1999), with methods of Steel and Torrie (1980), and differences among foliage species were determined using Duncan's multiple-range test (Duncan, 1955). Data on nutrient components of total feed intake, foliage consumed and digestibility were analyzed as 2×2 factorial experiments (2 animal species (sheep and goats) $\times$ 2 treatments (with or without PEG)) within each tree foliage for each experiment using 'PROC GLM' (SAS, 1999), with methods of Steel and Torrie (1980), to determine differences due to animal species and PEG. In the case of significant interactions (i.e., $P < 0.05$), Duncan's multiple-range test (Duncan, 1955) was used to separate means within animal species. Correlations between foliage secondary compounds (Table 6) used simple linear regression (SAS, 1999), whereas multiple regressions (Table 7) used the 'PROC STEPWISE' procedure of SAS (1999).

Example 3.

Here Is Some Additional Advice on Particular Problems Common to New Scientific Writers

Problem 1 [87]

The Methods section is prone to being wordy or overly detailed.

Avoid repeatedly using a single sentence to relate a single action; this results in very lengthy, wordy passages. A related sequence of actions can be combined into one sentence to improve clarity and readability:

Problematic Example: This is a very long and wordy description of a common, simple procedure. It is characterized by single actions per sentence and lots of unnecessary details.

> "The Petri dish was placed on the turntable. The lid was then raised slightly. An inoculating loop was used to transfer culture to the agar surface. The turntable was rotated 90 degrees by hand. The loop was moved lightly back and forth over the agar to spread the culture. The bacteria were then incubated at 37 C for 24 hr."

Improved Example: Same actions, but all the important information is given in a single, concise sentence. Note that superfluous detail and otherwise obvious information has been deleted while important missing information was added.

> "Each plate was placed on a turntable and streaked at opposing angles with fresh overnight E. coli culture using an inoculating loop. The bacteria were then incubated at 37 C for 24 hr."

Best: Here the author assumes the reader has basic knowledge of microbiological techniques and has deleted other superfluous information. The two sentences have been combined because they are related actions.

> "Each plate was streaked with fresh overnight E. coli culture and incubated at 37 C for 24 hr."

Problem 2 [87]

Avoid using ambiguous terms to identify controls or treatments, or other study parameters that require specific identifiers to be clearly understood.

Designators such as Tube 1, Tube 2, or Site 1 and Site 2 are completely meaningless out of context and difficult to follow in context.

Problematic example: In this example the reader will have no clue as to what the various tubes represent without having to constantly refer back to some previous point in the Methods.

> "A Spec 20 was used to measure A600 of Tubes 1, 2, and 3 immediately after chloroplasts were added (Time 0) and every 2 min. thereafter until the DCIP was completely reduced. Tube 4's A600 was measured only at Time 0 and at the end of the experiment."

Improved example: Notice how the substitution (in red) of treatment and control identifiers clarifies the passage both in the context of the paper, and if taken out of context.

> "A Spec 20 was used to measure A600 of the reaction mixtures exposed to light intensities of 1500, 750, and 350 uE/m2/sec immediately after chloroplasts were added (Time 0) and every 2 min. thereafter until the DCIP was completely reduced. The A600 of the no-light control was measured only at Time 0 and at the end of the experiment."

Chapter 4

RESULTS AND DISCUSSION

RESULTS SECTION [88,89]

The results section presents the findings of your study. It is important to plan this section carefully as it may contain a large amount of material which needs to be presented in an accessible, reader-friendly manner. This is a predominantly descriptive section, although in certain circumstances some commentary on the results may be appropriate. For example, it may be useful to indicate whether your results confirm your hypothesis, or whether they are similar to or significantly different from those of existing studies. The purpose of a results section is to present and illustrate your findings. Make this section a completely objective report of the results, and save all interpretation for the discussion. The results section normally contains tables and figures accompanied by text. Here is some advice on how to presents the results in this way:

- Decide which results need to be presented in tables or figures. For example, a table showing the gender distribution of the participants (male or female) is normally not necessary: this information can be presented clearly and succinctly in words only. However, results presenting more complex data or a larger number of variables should be presented numerically as well as in words.
- Decide how the results should be organized. For example, you could use your research questions as headings, presenting each set of results under the appropriate heading; or, if reporting the results of a survey, you could follow the order of the questions in the survey. In some

cases, it may be more appropriate to present the most important findings first.

- Use headings and sub-headings to make the structure of your results section more transparent and improve readability.
- Number all tables and figures and give each a title.
- When describing the content of a table or figure in the text, refer to the number of the table or figure. For example, 'Figure 1 shows....', or 'The results of ... are given in Table 2.
- Do not attempt to describe all the numeric information in a table or figure. The written text should highlight significant or interesting findings. However, in some cases it may be appropriate to state that certain findings are not significant; for example, if the findings do not support one of your hypotheses, you need to indicate this in the text.
- Do not discuss or interpret your results, report background information, or attempt to explain anything.
- Never include raw data or intermediate calculations in a research paper.
- Do not present the same data more than once.
- Text should complement any figures or tables, not repeat the same information.
- Please do not confuse figures with tables - there is a difference.
- The page length of this section is set by the amount and types of data to be reported. Continue to be concise, using figures and tables, if appropriate, to present results most effectively.

Important: You must clearly distinguish material that would normally be included in a research article from any raw data or other appendix material that would not be published. In fact, such material should not be submitted at all unless requested by the instructor.

Style [89]

- As always, use past tense when you refer to your results, and put everything in a logical order.
- In text, refer to each figure as "figure 1," "figure 2," etc.; number your tables as well (see the reference text for details).

- Place figures and tables, properly numbered, in order at the end of the report (clearly distinguish them from any other material such as raw data, standard curves, etc.).
- If you prefer, you may place your figures and tables appropriately within the text of your results section.

The function of the Results section is to objectively present your key results, *without* interpretation, in an orderly and logical sequence using both illustrative materials (Tables and Figures) and text. Summaries of the statistical analyses may appear either in the text (usually parenthetically) or in the relevant Tables or Figures (in the legend or as footnotes to the Table or Figure). The Results section should be organized around a series of Tables and/or Figures sequenced to present your key findings in a logical order. The text of the Results section follows this sequence and highlights the answers to the questions/hypotheses you investigated. Important negative results should be reported, too. Authors usually write the text of the results section based upon this sequence of Tables and Figures [90]. Write the text of the Results section concisely and objectively. The passive voice will likely dominate here, but use the active voice as much as possible. Use the past tense. Avoid repetitive paragraph structures. Do not interpret the data here. The transition into interpretive language can be a slippery slope [90,91]. Consider the following two examples:

- This example highlights the trend/difference that the author wants the reader to focus:

> The duration of exposure to running water had a pronounced effect on cumulative seed germination percentages (Figure 2). Seeds exposed to the 2-day treatment had the highest cumulative germination (84%), 1.25 times that of the 12-h or 5-day groups and 4 times that of controls.

- In contrast, this example strays subtly into interpretation by referring to optimality (a conceptual model) and teeing the observed result to that idea:

> The results of the germination experiment (Figure 2) suggest that the optimal time for running-water treatment is 2 days. This group showed the highest cumulative germination (84%), with longer (5 d) or shorter (12 h) exposures producing smaller gains in germination when compared to the control group.

Conditions

- Researchers should prepare the data in tables, figures, or diagrams according to the best method of presenting the data.
- Description the data obtained in the text should be depending on the statistical analysis (significant or no significant differences).
- Researcher should be focus in their description on the very important results obtained.
- If we have a data numerically higher, but not have significant differences, we can mention it in the text but with it P value.

o Example:
o "Addition of exogenous enzymes tended to P=0.231) increase VFA concentrations in the rumen of T1 than in T2 group"

- Results description could be divided in to sub-sections.
- Some journals prefer to write the results and discussion and the other no. generally we need to see how we can to write each section separately.
- Summarize your findings in text and illustrate them, if appropriate, with figures and tables.
- In text, describe each of your results, pointing the reader to observations that are most relevant.
- Provide a context, such as by describing the question that was addressed by making a particular observation.
- Describe results of control experiments and include observations that are not presented in a formal figure or table, if appropriate.
- Analyze your data, then prepare the analyzed (converted) data in the form of a figure (graph), table, or in text form.

STRATEGY FOR WRITING THE RESULTS SECTION

Remember that the Results section has both text and illustrative materials (Tables and Figures). Use the text component to guide the reader through your key results, i.e., those results which answer the question(s) you investigated. Each Table and Figure must be referenced in the text portion of the results, and you must tell the reader what the key result(s) is that each Table or Figure conveys.

THINGS TO CONSIDER AS YOU WRITE YOUR RESULTS SECTION [90,91]

What are the "Results"? When you pose a testable hypothesis that can be answered experimentally, or ask a question that can be answered by collecting samples, you accumulate observations about those organisms or phenomena. Those observations are then analyzed to yield an answer to the question. In general, the answer is the "key result".

The above statements apply regardless of the complexity of the analysis you employ. So, in an introductory course your analysis may consist of visual inspection of figures and simple calculations of means and standard deviations; in a later course you may be expected to apply and interpret a variety of statistical tests. You instructor will tell you the level of analysis that is expected.

For example, *suppose you asked the question, "Is the average height of male students the same as female students in a pool of randomly selected Biology majors?"* You would first collect height data from large random samples of male and female students. You would then calculate the descriptive statistics for those samples (mean, SD, n, range, etc) and plot these numbers. In a course where statistical tests are not employed, you would visually inspect these plots. Suppose you found that male Biology majors are, on average, 12.5 cm taller than female majors; this is the answer to the question.

- Notice that the outcome of a statistical analysis is not a key result, but rather an analytical *tool* that helps us understand *what is* our key result.

Organize the results section based on the sequence of Table and Figures you'll include. Prepare the Tables and Figures as soon as all the data are analyzed and arrange them in the sequence that best presents your findings in a logical way. A good strategy is to note, on a draft of each Table or Figure, the one or two key results you want to address in the text portion of the Results. Simple rules to follow related to Tables and Figures:

- Tables and Figures are assigned numbers separately and in the sequence that you will refer to them from the text.
    - o The first Table you refer to is Table 1, the next Table 2 and so forth.
    - o Similarly, the first Figure is Figure 1, the next Figure 2, etc.
- *Each* Table or Figure must include a brief description of the results being presented and other necessary information in a legend.
    - o *Table legends go above the Table*; tables are read from top to bottom.
    - o *Figure legends go below the figure*; figures are usually viewed from bottom to top.
- When referring to a Figure *from the text*, "Figure" is abbreviated as Figure, e.g., Figure 1. Table is never abbreviated, e.g., Table 1.

The body of the Results section is a text-based presentation of the key findings which includes references to each of the Tables and Figures. The text should guide the reader through your results stressing the key results which provide the answers to the question(s) investigated. A major function of the text is to provide clarifying information. You must refer to each Table and/or Figure individually and in sequence (see numbering sequence), and clearly indicate for the reader the key results that each conveys. Key results depend on your questions; they might include obvious trends, important differences, similarities, correlations, maximums, minimums, etc.

SOME PROBLEMS TO AVOID [90,91]

- *Do not* reiterate each value from a Figure or Table - only the key result or trends that each conveys.
- *Do not* present the same data in both a Table and Figure - this is considered redundant and a waste of space and energy. Decide which format best shows the result and go with it.
- *Do not* report raw data values when they can be summarized as means, percents, etc.

Statistical test summaries (test name, p-value) are usually reported parenthetically in conjunction with the biological results they support. Always report your results with parenthetical reference to the statistical conclusion that supports your finding (if statistical tests are being used in your course). This parenthetical reference should include the statistical test used and the level of significance (test statistic and DF are optional). For example, if you found that the mean height of male Biology majors was significantly larger than that of female Biology majors, you might report this result (in blue) and your statistical conclusion (shown in red) as follows:

> "Males (180.5 ± 5.1 cm; n=34) averaged 12.5 cm taller than females (168 ± 7.6 cm; n=34) in the AY 1995 pool of Biology majors (two-sample t-test, t = 5.78, 33 d.f., p < 0.001)."

If the summary statistics are shown in a figure, the sentence above need not report them specifically, but must include a reference to the figure where they may be seen:

> "Males averaged 12.5 cm taller than females in the AY 1995 pool of Biology majors (two-sample t-test, t = 5.78, 33 d.f., p < 0.001; Figure 1)."

Note that the report of the key result (shown in blue) would be identical in a paper written for a course in which statistical testing is not employed - the section shown in red would simply not appear except reference to the figure.

- Avoid devoting whole sentences to report a statistical outcome alone.
- Two notes about the use of the word significant(ly).
  - o In scientific studies, the use of this word implies that a statistical test was employed to make a decision about the data; in this case the test indicated a larger difference in mean heights than you would expect to get by chance alone. Limit the use of the word "significant" to this purpose only.
  - o If your parenthetical statistical information includes a p-value that is significant, it is unnecessary (and redundant) to use the word "significant" in the body of the sentence (see example above).

Present the results of your experiment(s) in a sequence that will logically support (or provide evidence against) the hypothesis, or answer the question, stated in the Introduction. For example, in reporting a study of the effect of an experimental diet on the skeletal mass of the rat, consider first giving the data on skeletal mass for the rats fed the control diet and then give the data for the rats fed the experimental diet.

Report Negative Results - they Are Important!

If you did not get the anticipated results, it may mean your hypothesis was incorrect and needs to be reformulated, or perhaps you have stumbled onto something unexpected that warrants further study. In either case, your results may be of importance to others even though they did not support your hypothesis. Do not fall into the trap of thinking that results contrary to what you expected are necessarily "bad data". If you carried out the work well, they are simply your results and need interpretation. Many important discoveries can be traced to "bad data".

Always Enter the Appropriate Units When Reporting Data or Summary Statistics [90,91]

- For an *individual value* you would write, "the mean length was 10 m", or, "the maximum time was 140 min".
- When including a measure of variability, place the unit *after* the error value, e.g., "...was 10 ± 2.3 m".
- Likewise place the unit after the last in a *series of numbers* all having the same unit. For example: "lengths of 5, 10, 15, and 20 m", or "no differences were observed after 2, 4, 6, or 8 min. of incubation".

A Strategy for Writing up Research Results [92]

Get Organized: Lists, Outlines, Notecards, etc. Before starting to write the paper, take the time to think about and develop a list of points to be made in the paper. As you progress, use whichever strategy works for you to begin to order and to organize those points and ideas into sections.

- *Balanced Review of the Primary Research Literature*: Do an in-depth, balanced review of the primary research literature relevant to your study questions prior to designing and carrying out the experiments. This review will help you learn what is known about the topic you are investigating and may let you avoid unnecessarily repeating work done by others. This literature will form the basis of your Introduction and Discussion. Training in *on-line searches* is available from the Reference Librarians. Do your search early enough to take advantage of the *Interlibrary Loan System* if need be.

- *Write the Introduction*: Once your hypothesis has been refined for testing, you will draft the Introduction to your paper. In PI courses you will bring a draft of the Introduction to lab the day of the experiment for critique by an instructor or TWA (Technical Writing Assistant).

- *Design and Conduct the Experiment:* Keep careful notes on procedures used during the experiment. You should write the Materials and Methods section upon completion of the experiment.

- *Analyze and Interpret the Results:* Once the data are collected, you must analyze and interpret the results. Analysis will include data summaries (e.g., calculating means and variances) and statistical tests to verify conclusions. Most scientists lay out their Tables and Figures upon completion of the data analysis before writing the Results section. Write the Table and Figure legends. It is good practice to note the one or two key results that each Table or Figure conveys and use this information as a basis for writing the Results section. Sequence and number the Tables and Figures in the order which best enables the reader to reach your conclusions.

- *Write the Results Section:* Remember that the Results section has both text and illustrative materials (Tables and Figures). Use the text component to guide the reader through your key results, i.e., those results which answer the question(s) you investigated. Each Table and Figure must be referenced in the text portion of the results, and you must tell the reader what the key result(s) is that each Table or Figure conveys.

- *Write the Discussion:* Interpretation of your results includes discussing how your results modify and fit in with what we previously understood about the problem.
  Review the literature again at this time. After completing the experiments you will have much greater insight into the subject, and by going through some of the literature again, information that seemed trivial before, or was overlooked, may tie something together and therefore prove very important to your own interpretation. Be sure to cite the works that you refer to.

- *Write the Abstract and Title:* The Abstract is always the last section written because it is a concise summary of the entire paper and should include a clear statement of your aims, a brief description of the methods, the key findings, and your interpretation of the key results.

The Title will probably be written earlier, but is often modified once the final form of the paper clearly known.

- *Self-Revise Your Paper:* Most authors revise their papers *at least* 2-3x before giving it out for peer review.
  Go back over your paper now and read it carefully; *read it aloud.* Does it say what you wanted it to say? Do any ideas, experiments, or interpretations need to be moved around within the text to enhance the logical flow of your arguments? Can you shorten long sentences to clarify them?
  - o Can you change passive verbs to active forms? Do the Tables and Figures have sufficient information to stand alone outside the context of the paper? Use your dictionary to correct spelling and your spell checker to catch typos.
- *Peer Review:* Have knowledgeable colleagues critique your paper. Use their comments to revise your paper yet again. Helpful documents:
  - o Making Effective Comments on Peer Reviews Peer Review Form
- *Prepare the Final Draft:* Carefully proof-read your final draft to make sure its as well done as possible.
  Double check that you've properly cited all your sources in the text and in the Literature Cited. Check the formatting one last time. The instructors LOVE to give full credit for format issues whenever possible, but will not hesitate to take points off for sloppy work.

TABLES AND FIGURES OF THE RESULTS SECTION [93]

Once your statistical analyses are complete, you will need to summarize the data and results for presentation to your readers. Data summaries may take one of 3 forms: text, Tables and Figures.

Text: contrary to what you may have heard, not all analyses or results warrant a Table or Figure. Some simple results are best stated in a single sentence, with data summarized parenthetically:

Seed production was higher for plants in the full-sun treatment (52.3 +/-6.8 seeds) than for those receiving filtered light (14.7+/- 3.2 seeds, t=11.8, df=55, p<0.001.)

General Conditions of Figures and Tables

- Either place figures and tables within the text of the result, or include them in the back of the report (following Literature Cited) - do one or the other
- If you place figures and tables at the end of the report, make sure they are clearly distinguished from any attached appendix materials, such as raw data
- Regardless of placement, each figure must be numbered consecutively and complete with caption (caption goes under the figure)
- Regardless of placement, each table must be titled, numbered consecutively and complete with heading (title with description goes above the table)
- Each figure and table must be sufficiently complete that it could stand on its own, separate from text

Tables: Tables present lists of numbers or text in columns, each column having a title or label. Do not use a table when you wish to show a trend or a pattern of relationship between sets of values - these are better presented in a Figure.

For instance, if you needed to present population sizes and sex ratios for your study organism at a series of sites, and you planned to focus on the differences among individual sites according to (say) habitat type, you would use a table.

However, if you wanted to show us that sex ratio was related to population size, you would use a Figure.

Figures: Figures are visual presentations of results, including graphs, diagrams, photos, drawings, schematics, maps, etc. Graphs are the most common type of figure and will be discussed in detail; examples of other types of figures are included at the end of this section. Graphs show trends or patterns of relationship.

Organizing your presentation: Once you have done your analyses and decided how best to present each one, think about how you will arrange them. Your analyses should tell a "story" which leads the reader through the steps needed to logically answer the question(s) you posed in your Introduction. The order in which you present your results can be as important in convincing your readers as what you actually say in the text.

How to refer to Tables and Figures from the text: Every Figure and Table included in the paper MUST be referred to from the text. Use sentences that draw the reader's attention to the relationship or trend you wish to highlight, referring to the appropriate Figure or Table only parenthetically:

> Germination rates were significantly higher after 24 h in running water than in controls (Figure 4).
> DNA sequence homologies for the purple gene from the four congeners (Table 1) show high similarity, differing by at most 4 base pairs.

Avoid sentences that give no information other than directing the reader to the Figure or Table:

> Table 1 shows the summary results for male and female heights at Bates College.

Abbreviation of the word "Figure": When referring to a Figure in the text, the word "Figure" is abbreviated as "Figure", while "Table" is not abbreviated. Both words are spelled out completely in descriptive legends.

How to number Tables and Figures: Figures and Tables are numbered *independently*, in the *sequence* in which you refer to them in the text, starting with Figure 1 and Table 1. If, in revision, you change the presentation sequence of the figures and tables, you must renumber them to reflect the new sequence.

Placement of Figures and Tables within the Paper: In manuscripts (e.g. lab papers, drafts), Tables and Figures are usually put on separate pages from text material. In consideration of your readers, place each Table or Figure as near as possible to the place where you first refer to it (e.g., the next page).

It is permissible to place all the illustrative material at the end of the Results section so as to avoid interrupting the flow of text.

The Figures and Tables may be embedded in the text, but avoid breaking up the text into small blocks; it is better to have whole pages of text with Figures and Tables on their own pages.

The "Acid Test" for Tables and Figures: Any Table or Figure you present must be sufficiently clear, well-labeled, and described by its legend to be understood by your intended audience without reading the results section, i.e., it must be able to stand alone and be interpretable.

Overly complicated Figures or Tables may be difficult to understand in or out of context, so strive for simplicity whenever possible.

If you are unsure whether your tables or figures meet these criteria, give them to a fellow biology major (not in your course) and ask them to interpret your results.

Descriptive Legends or Captions: To pass the "acid test" above, a clear and complete legend (sometimes called a caption) is essential. Like the title of the paper itself, each legend should convey as much information as possible about what the Table or Figure tells the reader:

- What results are being shown in the graph(s) including the summary statistics plotted
- The organism studied in the experiment (if applicable)
- Context for the results: the treatment applied or the relationship displayed, etc.
- Location (ONLY if a field experiment)
- Specific explanatory information needed to interpret the results shown (in tables, this is frequently done as footnotes)
- Culture parameters or conditions if applicable (temperature, media, etc) as applicable
- Sample sizes and statistical test summaries as they apply
- *Do not simply restate the axis labels with a "versus" written in between*

Example:

Figure 1. Height frequency (%) of White Pines (*Pinus strobus*) in the Thorncrag Bird Sanctuary, Lewiston, Maine, before and after the Ice Storm of '98. Before, n=137, after, n=133. Four trees fell during the storm and were excluded from the post-storm survey.

In the examples later in this section, note the completeness of the legends. When you are starting out, you can use one of these examples (or an appropriate example from a published paper) as a model to follow in constructing your own legends.

NOTE: Questions frequently arise about how much methodology to include in the legend, and how much results reporting should be done.

For lab reports, specific results should be reported in the results text with a reference to the applicable Table or Figure. Other than culture conditions, methods are simmilarly confined to the Methods section.

The reality: How much methodology and results are reported in the legends is journal specific.

Hot-off-the-press journals like *Science* and *Nature* so limit the body text that virtually all of the Methods are presented in the Figure and Table legends or in footnotes.

Much of the results are also reported in the legends.

Where Do You Place the Legend? [93]

- Table legends go above the body of the Table and are left justified; Tables are read from the top down.
- Figure legends go below the graph; graphs and other types of Figures are usually read from the bottom up.

The Anatomy of a Table [93]

Table 4 below shows the typical layout of a table in three sections demarcated by lines. Tables are most easily constructed using your word processor's table function or a spread sheet such as Excel. Gridlines or boxes, commonly invoked by word processors, are optional for our purposes, but unlikely to be permitted in a journal.

Table 4 Population variation in hatch success (mean percent) of unfertilized eggs for females from populations sampled in 1997. N = number of females tested. **<--Table legend**

Population	mean (%)	Standard deviation	Range	N
Beaver Creek [T]	7.31	13.95	0-53.16	15
Honey Creek [T]	4.33	7.83	0-25.47	11
Rock Bridge Gans Creek [T]	5.66	13.93	0-77.86	38
Cedar Creek [P]	6.56	9.64	0-46.52	64
Grindstone Creek [P]	8.56	14.77	0-57.32	19
Jacks Fork River [P]	5.28	8.28	0-30.96	28
Meramec River [P]	5.49	10.25	0-45.76	45
Little Dixie Lake [L]	7.96	14.54	0-67.66	71
Little Prairie Lake [L]	6.86	7.84	0-32.40	36
Rocky Forks Lake [L]	3.31	4.12	0-16.14	43
Winegar Lake [L]	10.73	17.58	0-41.64	5
Whetstone Lake [L]	7.36	12.93	0-63.38	57

<--Column titles

<--Table body (data)

[T] = temporary stream, [P] = permanent streams, [L] = lakes. **<--footnotes**

<--Lines demarcating the different parts of the table

Example 1. Courtesy of Shelley Ball [93].

Table 2. Log-likelihood tests of deviation from 1:1 sex ratios for nymphs collected from each population in 1997 and 1998. Values are ratios of female:male; sample sizes are in parentheses. Bonferroni corrected probabilities are shown with an asterisks.

	Year	
Population	1997	1998
Beaver Creek[T]	9.00:1(20)***	2.67:1 (22)*
Honey Creek[T]	9.00:1(56)***	2.27:1 (98)***
Rock Bridge[T]	3.33:1(26)**	2.09:1 (68)**
Cedar Creek[P]	2.05:1(119)***	1.87:1 (198)***
Grindstone Creek[P]	-	2.26:1 (140)***
Jacks Fork River[P]	2.89:1(35)**	5.17:1 (37)***
Meramec River[P]	2.80:1(38)**	2.41:1 (58)**
Little Dixie Lake[L]	2.45:1(494)***	2.46:1 (384)***
Little Prairie Lake[L]	2.38:1 (71)***	2.08:1 (157)***
Rocky Forks Lake[L]	2.55:1 (213)***	2.93:1 (299)***
Winegar Lake[L]	3.41:1 (207)***	2.34:1 (204)***
Whetstone Lake[L]	2.69:1 (381)***	2.01:1 (268)***

* significant at $p < 0.05$; ** significant at $p < 0.005$; *** significant at $p < 0.001$.
[T] = temporary stream, [P] = permanent streams, [L] = lakes.

Example 2. Courtesy of Shelley Ball [93].

Table 2. Planting date, mean planting density, and total number of seed clams planted in plots at Filucy Bay and Wescott Bay in 1979.

Location	Plot code	Planting date	Mean planting density in no. clams/m^2 ± 1 st. dev.(N)	Total no. clams planted
Filucy Bay	F10 x 30	5-16-79	994 ± 39(5)	298200
	F3 x 10	5-24-79	994 ± 39(5)	29820
Wescott Bay	W10 x 25	5-16-79	994 ± 39(5)	248500
	W3 x 10	6-2-79	895 ± 35(5)[a]	26850

[a]Calculated after clams were planted based on estimated 11% mortality of seed clams between 5-24 and 6-2-79.

Example 3: Courtesy of Greg Anderson [93].

In these examples notice several things:

- The presence of a period *after* "Table #"
- The legend goes *above* the Table
- *Units* are specified in column headings wherever appropriate
- Lines of demarcation are used to set legend, headers, data, and footnotes apart from one another
- *Footnotes* are used to clarify points in the table, or to convey repetitive information about entries
- Footnotes may also be used to denote statistical differences among groups

The Anatomy of a Figure [93]

The sections below show when and how to use the four most common Figure types (bar graph, frequency histogram, XY scatterplot, XY line graph.) The final section gives examples of other, less common, types of Figures.

Parts of a Graph: Below are example figures (typical line and bar graphs) with the various component parts labeled in red.

Refer back to these examples if you encounter an unfamiliar term as you read the following sections.

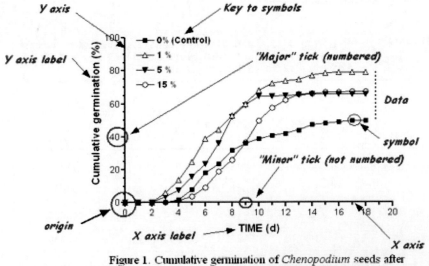

Figure 1. Cumulative germination of *Chenopodium* seeds after pregermination treatment of 2 day soak in NaCl solutions. n = 1 trial per treatment group (100 seeds/trial.)

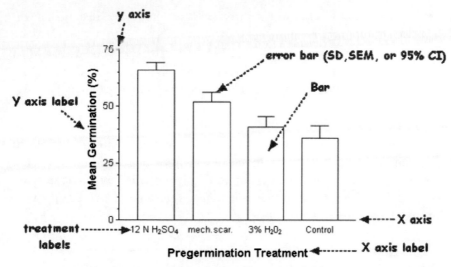

Figure 1. Mean germination (%) of gourd seeds following various pregermination treatments. N=10 groups of 100 seeds per treatment and control. Treatments: 12 hour soak in 12 N H_2SO_4, 90 second scarification of seed coat with 80 grit sandpaper, 6 hour soak in 3% H_2O_2.

Some General Considerations about Figures [93]

- *Big or little?* For course-related papers, a good rule of thumb is to size your figures to fill about one-half of a page. Readers should not have to reach for a magnifying glass to make out the details.
- *Color or no color?* Most often black and white is preferred. The rationale is that if you need to photocopy or fax your paper, any information conveyed by colors will be lost to the reader. However, for a poster presentation or a talk with projected images, color can be helpful in distinguishing different data sets. Every aspect of your Figure should convey information; *never use color simply because it is pretty.*
- *Title or no title? Never use a title for Figures included in a paper;* the legend conveys all the necessary information and the title just takes up extra space. However, *for posters or projected images*, where people may have a harder time reading the small print of a legend, a larger font title is very helpful.

- *Offset axes or not?* Elect to offset the axes only when data points will be obscured by being printed over the Y axis.
- *Error bars or not?* Always include error bars (SD or SEM) when plotting means. In some courses you may be asked to plot other measures associated with the mean, such as confidence intervals.

Compound Figures [93]

Compound figures combine multiple graphs into one common figure and share a common legend. Each figure must be identified by letter (A, B, C, etc), and, when referred to from the text, is specifically identified by that letter, e.g., "...(*Figure 1b*)". The legend of the compound figure must also identify each graph and the data it presents by letter.

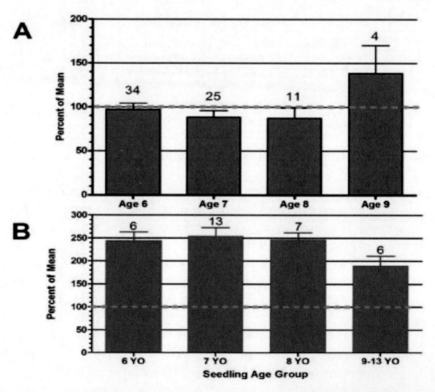

Figure 3. Age-specific primary growth of seedling white pine in the harvest zone in (A) 2006 and (B) 2007, relative to the mean primary growth increments of the three years ('03-'05) prior to the selective harvest. Data shown are the mean (SEM); number over bar is number of seedlings. Dashed line at 100% indicates level where post-harvest growth equals mean pre-harvest growth [93].

FOUR COMMON FIGURE TYPES [93]

Bar Graph

Bar graphs are used when you wish to compare the value of a single variable (usually a summary value such as a mean) among several groups. For example, a bar graph is appropriate to show the mean sizes of plants harvested from plots that received 4 different fertilizer treatments. (Note that although a bar graph might be used to show differences between only 2 groups, especially for pedagogical purposes, editors of many journals would prefer that you save space by presenting such information in the text).

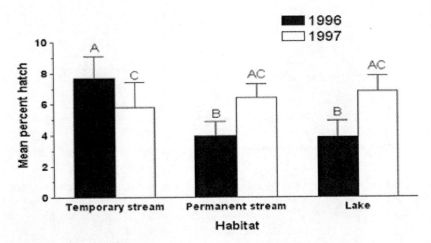

Figure 3. Effects of habitant and year on tychoparthenogenetic capacity (mean % hatching success ± 1SD of unfertilized eggs) in mayflies. Means with different letters are significantly different (Turkey's HSD, p.<0.05) [93].

In this example notice that:

- Legend goes *below* the figure
- A period follows "Figure 1" and the legend itself; "Figure" is not abbreviated
- The *measured* variable is labelled on the Y axis. In most cases units are given here as well (see next example)
- The *categorical* variable (habitat) is labelled on the X axis, and each category is designated

- A *second* categorical variable (year) within habitat has been designated by *different bar fill patterns*. The patterns *must* be defined in a *key*, located wherever there is a convenient space within the graph
- Error bars are included, extending +1 SD or SEM above the mean
- Statistical differences may be indicated by a system of letters above the bars, with an accompanying note in the caption indicating the test and the significance level used.

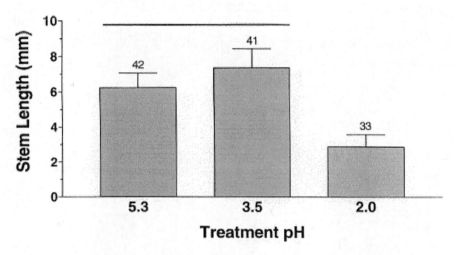

Figure 1. Mean stem length (±1SD) of seedling clover waters to soil saturation daily for 2.5 weeks with simulated acid rain of varying pH. The control (pH 5.3) was normal city tapwater. The pH3.5 and 2.0 water was acidified with 2M sulfuric/1M nitric acid solution. Line over bars indicated groups which were not significantly different (kruskal-Wallis Test and Dunn's Multiple Comparison's tests). Number over bar indicates sample size [93].

Notice Here

- The completeness of the legend, which in this case requires over 3 lines just to describe the treatments used and variable measured
- Axis labels, with units
- Treatment group (pH) levels specified on X axis
- Error bars and group sample sizes accompany each bar, and each of these is well-defined in legend

- Statistical differences in this case are indicated by lines drawn over the bars, and the statistical test and significance level are identified in the legend.

Frequency Histogram [93]

Frequency histograms (also called frequency distributions) are bar-type graphs that show how the measured individuals are distributed along an axis of the measured variable. Frequency (the Y axis) can be *absolute* (i.e. number of counts) or *relative* (i.e. percent or proportion of the sample.) A familiar example would be a histogram of exam scores, showing the number of students who achieved each possible score. Frequency histograms are important in describing populations, e.g. size and age distributions.

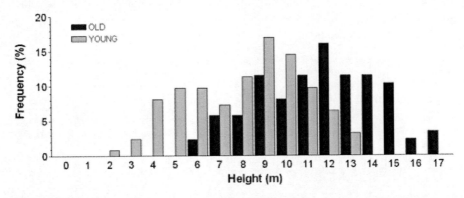

Figure 4. Height distriction in two recruitment cohorts of eastern white pine (Pinus strobes) near the eastern shore of lake Auburn, Maine, in januray 2001. N=88OLD and 123 YOUNG trees [93].

Notice several things about this example:

- The Y axis includes a clear indication ("%") that relative frequencies are used. (Some examples of an absolute frequencies: "Number of stems", "Number of birds observed")
- The measured variable (X axis) has been divided into categories ("bins") of appropriate width to visualize the population distribution. In this case, bins of 0.2 cm broke the population into 7 columns of varying heights. Setting the bin size at 0.5 cm would have yielded only 3 columns, not enough to visualize a pattern. Conversely, setting

the bin size too small (0.05 cm) would have yielded very short columns scattered along a long axis, again obscuring the pattern

- The values labeled on the X axis are the bin *centers*
- Sample size is clearly indicated, either in the legend or (in this case) the graph itself
- The Y axis includes numbered and minor ticks to allow easy determination of bar values

X, Y Scatterplot

These are plots of X,Y coordinates showing each individual's or sample's score on *two* variables.

When plotting data this way we are usually interested in knowing whether the two variables show a "relationship", i.e. do they change in value together in a consistent way?

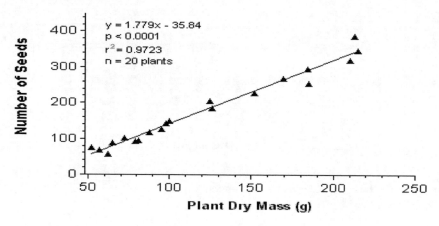

Figure 5. Seed production as a function of plant biomass in waterlilies (Nuphar luteum) harvested from Great Works Pond in Northern maine in August 2001 [93].

Note in this example that:

- Each axis is labeled (including units where appropriate) and includes numbered and minor ticks to allow easy determination of the values of plotted points
- Sample size is included in the legend or the body of the graph
- If the data have been analyzed statistically and a relationship between the variables exists, it may be indicated by plotting the regression line

on the graph, and by giving the equation of the regression and its
statistical significance in the legend or body of the figure

- The range of each axis has been carefully selected to maximize the
spread of the points and to minimize wasted blank space where no
points fall.
For instance, the X axis is truncated below 50 g because no plants
smaller than 52 g were measured. The ranges selected also result in
labeled ticks that are easy to read (50, 100, 150..., rather than 48, 96,
144...)

Which variable goes on the X axis? When one variable is clearly
dependent upon another (e.g. height depends on age, but it is hard to imagine
age depending on height), the convention is to plot the *dependent variable on
the Y axis and the independent variable on the X axis.*

Sometimes there is no clear independent variable (e.g. length vs. width of
leaves: does width depend on width, or vice-versa?) In these cases it makes no
difference which variable is on which axis; the variables are inter-dependent,
and an X,Y plot of these shows the *relationship* BETWEEN them (rather than
the effect of one upon the other.)

In the example plotted above, we can imagine that seed production *might*
depend on plant biomass, but it is hard to see how biomass could depend
directly on seed production, so we choose biomass as the X axis.
Alternatively, the relationship might be indirect: *both* seed production *and*
plant biomass might depend on some other, unmeasured variable. Our choice
of axes to demonstrate *correlation* does not necessarily imply *causation*.

X, Y Line Graph [93]

Line graphs plot a series of related values that depict a change in Y as a
function of X. Two common examples are a growth curve for an individual or
population over time, and a dose-response curve showing effects of increasing
doses of a drug or treatment.

When to connect the dots? If each point in the series is obtained from the
same source and is dependent on the previous values (e.g. a plot of a baby's
weight over the course of a year, or of muscle strength on successive
contractions as a muscle fatigues), then the points should be connected by a
line in a dot-to-dot fashion.

If, however, the series represents independent measurements of a variable
to show a trend (e.g. mean price of computer memory over time; a standard
curve of optical density vs. solute concentration), then the trend or relationship

can be modeled by calculating the best-fit line or curve by regression analysis (*see A Painless Guide to Statistics* [94]) *Do not connect the dots* when the measurements were made independently.

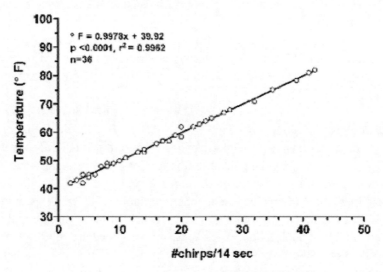

Figure 6. Temperature-dependence of cricket chirp frequency in south central Maine. Temperature (F) = #chirps in 14 sec+40. n=36 cricket chirp bouts [93].

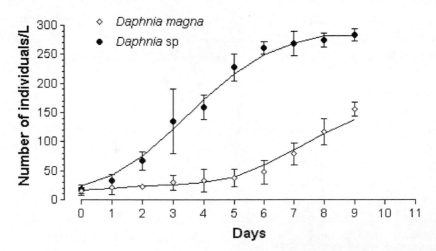

Figure 7. mean population density (±1 standard deviation) of two species of Daphnia following artificial eutrophication of a small farm pond by application of organic fertilizer. Six replicate 1 L water samples were drawn from 50cm depth at 1100 hr each day [93].

In this example notice:

- A different symbol is used for each group (species), and the key to the symbols is placed in the body of the graph where space permits. Symbols are large enough to be easily recognizable in the final graph size
- Each point represents a mean value, and this is stated in the legend. Error bars are therefore plotted for each point and defined in the legend as well
- Because measurements were taken on independent groups for each species, the points are NOT connected dot-to-dot; instead a curve is fitted to the data to show the trend

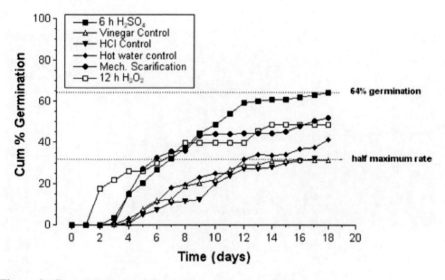

Figure 8. Cumulative germination of gourd seeds following various pregermination treatments n= 100 seeds per trial [93].

Notice here that:

- This time the dots ARE connected dot-to-dot within each treatment, because cumulative percent germination was measured within the same set of seeds each day, and thus is *dependent* on the measurements of the prior days

- A different symbol is used for each treatment, and symbols are large enough (and connecting lines fine enough) so that all can be easily read at the final graph size
- In addition to the key to symbols, two other kinds of helpful information are supplied in the body of the figure: the values of the highest and lowest final cumulative percents, and a dashed line (baseline) showing the lowest cumulative % germination achieved. This baseline is defined in the legend

Some Other Types of Figures [101]

Photographs

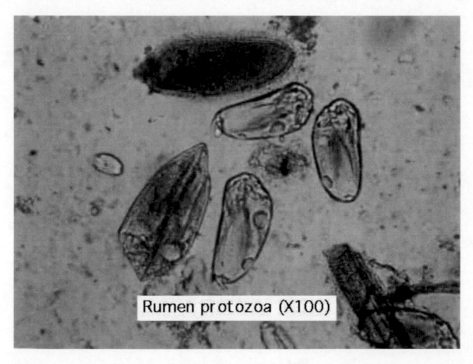

Rumen protozoa (X100)

Figure 9. A microscopic photo of the rumen protozoa [101].

Notice here that:

- A photograph is a *figure.*
- Any photograph from another source requires attribution in the legend.
- Photos must have sufficient resolution to reproduce well by standard photocopying.

Gels [95]

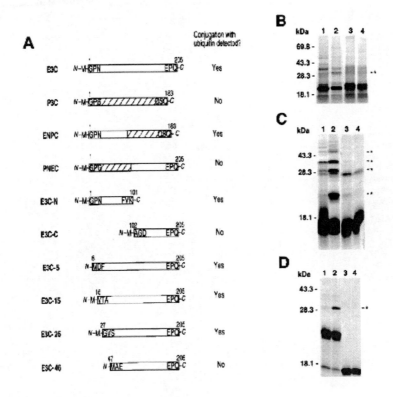

EXAMPLES OF THE RESULTS TEXT

NOTE:

- Divided the results section to many sub-sections
- Writing the scientific names

3. Results

3.1. Chemical composition and secondary compounds of the tree foliages

The crude protein (CP) content of the foliages (Table 1) ranged from 124 (*S. molle*) and 128 (*C. speciosa*) to 185 g/kg DM (*C. fistula*), with *E. camaldulensis* intermediate (154 g/kg). Ether extract was highest (97 g/kg) in *S. molle*, with the others containing less than half that level. *C. fistula* had the lowest NDFom, ADFom and lignin(sa), *E. camaldulensis* had the highest values, and *S. molle* and *C. speciosa* were intermediate.

Total phenolics, condensed tannins, saponins, alkaloids, the aqueous fraction of lectins, polypeptides and starch, and essential oils were lowest in *C. speciosa* (29, 21, 3, 0, 4 g/kg DM and 0.40 ml/kg DM, respectively) and highest in *E. camaldulensis* (102, 68, 15, 5, 3 and 15). *C. fistula* and *S. molle* had intermediate values, although *S. molle* had higher levels of TP and CT. Tannins (*i.e.*, TP and CT) were higher than 50 g/kg of DM in *S. molle* (70

Table 1
Nutrient and secondary compound levels (g/kg DM) of foliages and the concentrate

	Tree species				S.E.M.	Concentrate[a]
	C. fistula	*S. molle*	*C. speciosa*	*E. camaldulensis*		
Chemical composition[b]						
OM	923 b	909 d	916 c	945 a	0.88	965 (0.6)
CP	185 a	124 d	128 c	154 b	0.95	147 (2.3)
EE	39 c	97 a	47 b	41 bc	2.64	83 (1.2)
NDFom	368 d	515 b	435 c	615 a	4.47	289 (3.4)
ADFom	200 d	327 c	356 b	542 a	5.56	186 (2.1)
Lignin(sa)	101 c	160 b	102 c	192 a	2.82	110 (1.8)
Secondary compounds[c]						
TP	44.3 c	67.7 b	29.0 d	102.3 a	2.76	12.4 (1.6)
CT	31.6 c	49.2 b	20.8 d	68.1 a	0.96	ND[d]
SAP	8.3 b	10.3 b	3.0 c	14.6 a	0.73	ND
ALKA	1.3 b	1.9 b	0.0 c	5.0 a	0.20	ND
AF	8.6 a	6.6 b	3.9 c	2.4 d	0.28	ND
EO	0.8 c	5.3 b	0.4 c	15.5 a	0.27	ND

In the same row with different online letters (a, b, c, d) differ (P<0.05).

[a] Mean value ± S.D.

[b] OM, organic matter; CP, crude protein; EE, ether extract; NDFom, neutral detergent fiber; ADFom, acid detergent fiber; lignin(sa), acid detergent lignin.

[c] TP, total extractable phenolic components; CT, condensed tannins (as quebracho equivalent); SAP, saponins; ALKA, alkaloids; AF, aqueous fraction (lectins, polypeptides, starch; Cowan, 1999); EO, essential oils (ml/kg DM).

[d] Assumed to be zero (<0.01 g/kg DM).

and 50) and *E. camaldulensis* (110 and 70), which is considered to be their upper beneficial level in ruminant nutrition (Mangan, 1988).

Example 1. (to be continued).

3.2. Effects of tree foliage species on intake and digestion

3.2.1. C. fistula

Water consumption was higher (P<0.05) in sheep, although the actual values are not convincing. Sheep also consumed more (P<0.01) total and foliage DM (absolutely and relative to BW) than goats (Table 2), as well as all measured nutrients, although their digestion of nutrients, except NDFom, was lower (P<0.05).

Addition of PEG had no impact on water intake, but increased (P<0.05) intake of DM and its components in sheep and goats. Digestion of DM and NDFom were not affected by feeding PEG, although digestion of OM, EE and CP were higher (P<0.05).

3.2.2. S. molle

Water consumption was higher (P<0.05) in sheep, which consumed more (P<0.01) total, but not foliage, DM (absolute and relative to BW) than goats (Table 3), as well as all measured nutrients, although their digestion of nutrients, except NDFom, was lower (P<0.05).

Addition of PEG had no impact on water intake, but increased (P<0.05) intake of DM and its components absolutely, although relative to BW the increase in DM intake and digestibility was greater within goats (P=0.04). Digestion of DM and NDFom were not

Table 2
Water intake (l/d), feed intake (g/d) and digestion (g/kg) in sheep and goats fed *C. fistula* in the absence (−) or presence (+) of PEG

Species (Sp)	Sheep		Goats		S.E.M.	Significance (P)		
PEG	−	+	−	+		Sp	PEG	Sp × PEG
Water intake (l/d)	2.3	3.0	2.5	2.5	0.08	0.01	0.40	0.65
Dry matter (DM) intake								
Foliage (g/d)	309	329	262	272	4.2	<0.01	0.03	0.41
Foliage (g/kg$^{0.75}$)	21.4	22.9	20.4	21.2	0.31	0.02	0.03	0.48
Concentrate[a]	320	320	274	274				
Total (g/d)	629	649	536	546	4.2	<0.01	0.03	0.41
Total (g/kg$^{0.75}$)	43.8	45.2	41.9	42.6	0.31	<0.01	0.03	0.48
DM digestion	502	525	549	565	4.6	0.01	0.25	0.06
Organic matter								
Intake	594	613	507	516	3.9	<0.01	0.03	0.41
Digestion	531	547	579	595	4.0	<0.01	0.02	0.98
Ether extract								
Intake	26	27	22	23	0.2	<0.01	0.03	0.41
Digestion	527	556	556	570	6.1	0.04	0.04	0.41
Crude protein								
Intake	104	108	89	91	0.8	<0.01	0.03	0.41
Digestion	521	536	565	606	7.2	<0.01	0.02	0.23
Neutral detergent fiber								
Intake	206b	214a	132b	179a	1.4	<0.01	<0.01	<0.01
Digestion	448	468	464	482	7.3	0.20	0.10	0.92

In the same row (within animal species) with different letters (a, b) differ (P<0.05).
[a] Concentrate intake was not statistically analyzed as it was offered at a flat rate.

affected by feeding PEG, although digestion of OM, EE and CP were higher (P<0.05) with PEG feeding.

Example 1. (to be continued).

3.2.3. C. speciosa

Water consumption was higher (P=0.02) in sheep, which consumed more (P<0.01) total and foliage DM than goats absolutely (but less (P<0.01) foliage than goats relative to BW) (Table 4), as well as all measured nutrients, although their digestion of nutrients, except CP and NDFom, was lower (P<0.05 except OM P=0.06).

Addition of PEG had no impact on water intake, but increased (P<0.05) intake of DM and its components both absolutely and relative to BW, although relative to BW the increase in total DM intake was greater within goats (P=0.01). Digestion of CP and NDFom were not affected by feeding PEG, although digestion of DM, OM and EE were higher (P<0.05) with PEG feeding.

3.2.4. E. camaldulensis

Water consumption was unaffected by animal species, but sheep consumed more (P<0.01) total, but not foliage, DM than goats absolutely (although goats consumed more

Table 3

Water intake (l/d), feed intake (g/d) and digestion (g/kg) in sheep and goats fed *S. molle* in the absence (−) or presence (+) of PEG

	Sheep		Goats		S.E.M.	Significance (P)		
	−	+	−	+		Sp	PEG	Sp × PEG
Water intake (l/d)	3.6	3.1	2.9	2.8	0.1	0.04	0.25	0.90
Dry matter (DM) intake								
Foliage (g/d)	269	316	259	331	4.9	0.75	<0.01	0.11
Foliage (g/kg$^{0.75}$)	18.7 b	22.0 a	20.2 b	25.8 a	0.35	<0.01	<0.01	0.04
Concentrate[a]	320	320	274	274				
Total (g/d)	589	636	533	605	4.9	0.02	0.01	0.11
Total (g/kg$^{0.75}$)	41.0 b	44.3 a	41.6 b	47.2 a	0.35	0.01	<0.01	0.04
DM digestion	505	506	529	544	4.3	<0.01	0.19	0.13
Organic matter								
Intake	554	596	500	566	4.5	<0.01	<0.01	0.11
Digestion	538	544	567 b	605 a	6.2	<0.01	0.02	0.04
Ether extract								
Intake	40	44	37	44	0.5	0.03	<0.01	0.11
Digestion	511	536	544	559	5.8	0.01	0.04	0.54
Crude protein								
Intake	80	86	72	81	0.6	<0.01	<0.01	0.11
Digestion	496	528	544	608	6.2	<0.01	<0.01	0.10
Neutral detergent fiber								
Intake	231 b	225 a	164 b	250 a	2.5	<0.01	<0.01	<0.01
Digestion	491	503	496	522	7.5	0.29	0.11	0.52

In the same row (within animal species) with different letters (a, b) differ (P<0.05).

[a] Concentrate intake was not statistically analyzed as it was offered at a flat rate.

(P=0.01) foliage DM relative to BW) (Table 5), as well as all measured nutrients, although their digestion of nutrients was lower (P<0.05 except EE P=0.06).

Addition of PEG tended (P=0.06) to increase water consumption, although the actual values are not convincing. Addition of PEG only increased (P<0.05) intake of NDFom, although intake of DM and all other measured components tended (P<0.10) to be higher. Digestion of EE and NDFom were not affected by PEG, although digestion of DM, OM and CP were higher (P<0.05 except DM P=0.07) with PEG.

Example 1.

Table 2

In situ degradability (g/kg) of dry matter (DMD), crude protein (CPD), neutral detergent fiber (NDFD) and acid detergent fiber (ADFD) of some browse tree foliages after 48 h of incubation in the rumen of cows as well as unadapted (UG) and adapted (AG) goats during the rainy and dry seasons.

Season	Inoculum	Browse	DMD	CPD	NDFD	ADFD
Rainy	Cows	L. acapulcencis	241.6^k	21.7^l	61.1^{ij}	109.3^{hk}
		Q. laeta	331.8^{gh}	131.4^{hi}	142.0^{ef}	230.7^{ef}
		P. dulce	544.3^c	584.6^{bc}	308.6^{bc}	303.6^{cd}
	UG	L. acapulcencis	273.1^{ij}	19.9^j	88.0^{iv}	121.2^{hs}
		Q. laeta	369.5^{ef}	176.0^{hg}	162.5^{ef}	247.6^{ef}
		P. dulce	547.8^c	581.9^{bc}	332.4^{ab}	374.7^{ab}
	AG	L. acapulcencis	281.9^j	108.5^{ij}	109.2^{ijg}	144.3^{gh}
		Q. laeta	389.5^e	226.4^f	163.7^{ef}	198.5^{fg}
		P. dulce	514.6^d	563.1^c	273.8^c	340.2^{bc}
Dry	Cows	L. acapulcencis	296.7^{ij}	59.0^{kl}	38.1^j	61.6^i
		Q. laeta	499.9^d	214.0^f	121.1^{gh}	112.5^{hk}
		P. dulce	596.9^b	625.4^b	214.7^d	291.5^{cde}
	UG	L. acapulcencis	310.7^{ih}	71.2^{jk}	77.6^{hij}	101.5^{hk}
		Q. laeta	551.7^c	304.8^e	217.0^d	143.9^{gh}
		P. dulce	668.9^a	730.9^a	366.2^a	404.1^a
	AG	L. acapulcencis	344.7^{ef}	152.1^{hi}	116.1^{efh}	121.7^{hk}
		Q. laeta	558.6^c	371.6^d	197.7^{ed}	105.2^{hk}
		P. dulce	652.8^a	738.5^a	336.2^{ab}	381.8^{ab}
Sed	5.61	9.73		9.84	10.92	

	P value			
	DMD	CPD	NDFD	ADFD
Season	<0.001	<0.001	0.232	<0.001
Inoculum	<0.001	<0.001	<0.001	<0.001
Browse	<0.001	<0.001	<0.001	<0.001
Season × inoculum × browse	<0.001	<0.001	<0.001	<0.001

UG: unadapted goats; AG: adapted goats. Means within a column with different superscripts differ (P<0.05).

3. Results

The CP content of the browse species ranged from 85 g/kg (DS: dry season) and 94 g/kg (RS: rainy season) for Q. Laeta to 262 g/kg DM for P. dulce in the RS (Table 1). Overall, CP content of browse species was considerably higher in the rainy season (P<0.001). P. dulce had the lowest NDFom and ADFom in the two seasons, L. acapulcencis had the highest values, and Q. laeta values were intermediate with an overall increase in fiber fractions in the rainy season (P<0.001). The browse species differed in CT contents (P<0.01—Table 1). Overall, free-CT values were lower in Q. Laeta and P. dulce in the RS than in the DS, except L. acapulcencis had the opposite though non-significant effect. Soluble or free-CT fraction varied from 36.6 in P. dulce to 116.3 g/kg DM in L. acapulcencis during the RS. The protein-bound CT (PCT) fraction had the same trend of free-CT content in the tree species and varied (P<0.05) from 21 g/kg in P. dulce (DS) to 67.8 g/kg DM in L. acapulcencis (RS). PCT was not different between Q. Laeta and P. dulce in the two seasons.

Season of harvest (RS or DS), and ruminal inoculum (cows, goats (UG or AG)) both affected (P<0.001) DMD, CPD and fiber fractions of the browse (Table 2). Nutrient in situ degradability of all browse species was higher (P<0.001) during the DS than the RS. In situ degradability of browse species in goats previously exposed to the browse species (AG) was higher (P<0.001) than in cows or UG fed diets without browse. Overall, goats had higher (P<0.001) nutrient degradability of browse foliage than cows. However, P. dulce had the highest (P<0.001) in situ degradability values, while the lowest values were for L. acapulcencis with Q. laeta intermediate during the two growing seasons.

Example 2.

DISCUSSION
(INTERPRETATIONS OF THE RESULTS)

Journal guidelines vary. Space is so valuable in the Journal of Biological Chemistry, that authors are asked to restrict discussions to four pages or less, double spaced, typed. That works out to one printed page. While you are learning to write effectively, the limit will be extended to five typed pages. If you practice economy of words that should be plenty of space within which to say all that you need to say [89]. The objective here is to provide an interpretation of your results and support for all of your conclusions, using evidence from your experiment and generally accepted knowledge, if appropriate. The significance of findings should be clearly described [89]. The function of the Discussion is to interpret your results in light of what was already known about the subject of the investigation, and to explain our new understanding of the problem after taking your results into consideration. The Discussion will always connect to the Introduction by way of the question(s) or hypotheses you posed and the literature you cited, but it does not simply repeat or rearrange the Introduction. Instead, it tells how your study has moved us forward from the place you left us at the end of the Introduction [90].

Fundamental Questions to Answer Here Include [89]

- Do your results provide answers to your testable hypotheses? If so, how do you interpret your findings?
- Do your findings agree with what others have shown? If not, do they suggest an alternative explanation or perhaps a unforeseen design flaw in your experiment (or theirs?)
- Given your conclusions, what is our new understanding of the problem you investigated and outlined in the Introduction?
- If warranted, what would be the next step in your study, e.g., what experiments would you do next?

Strategies [89]

- Usually use the possibility words such "*may be, might be, could be*" and then due to the explanation.
- Use the active voice whenever possible in this section. Watch out for wordy phrases; be concise and make your points clearly. Use of the first person is okay, but too much use of the first person may actually distract the reader from the main points.
- Organize the Discussion to address each of the experiments or studies for which you presented results; discuss each in the same sequence as presented in the Results, providing your interpretation of what they mean in the larger context of the problem. Do not waste entire

sentences restating your results; if you need to remind the reader of the result to be discussed, use "bridge sentences" that relate the result to the interpretation:

> "The slow response of the lead-exposed neurons relative to controls suggests that...[interpretation]".

- You will necessarily make reference to the findings of others in order to support your interpretations. Use subheadings, if need be, to help organize your presentation. Be wary of mistaking the reiteration of a result for an interpretation, and make sure that no new results are presented here that rightly belong in the results. Use the previous studies to confirm the current results obtained, for example:
  1. Our results >>>> a finding consistent with Gilboa et al. (1995) who found that goats were able to consume larger amounts of tannin-rich browse than sheep under similar conditions, probably due, at least partially, to the ability of goats to detoxify higher amounts of tannins or secondary compounds *versus* other ruminants (Silanikove et al., 1996)
  2. Our explanation (References)
  3. Example: Goats, as browsers, may have selected the parts of the foliage with a lower proportion of secondary compounds, *versus* sheep as grazers (Kababya et al., 1998; Salem, 2002; Salem et al., 2003)
  4. Feeding PEG has been shown to improve intake of foliage containing secondary compounds in goats (Silanikove et al., 1997; Decandia et al., 2000) and sheep (Silanikove et al., 1994; Salawu et al., 1997)
- You must relate your work to the findings of other studies - including previous studies you may have done and those of other investigators. As stated previously, you may find crucial information in someone else's study that helps you interpret your own data, or perhaps you will be able to reinterpret others' findings in light of yours. In either case you should discuss reasons for similarities and differences between yours and others' findings. Consider how the results of other studies may be combined with yours to derive a new or perhaps better substantiated understanding of the problem. Be sure to state the conclusions that can be drawn from your results in light of these considerations. You may also choose to briefly mention further

studies you would do to clarify your working hypotheses. Make sure to reference any outside sources as shown in the Introduction section.

- Do not introduce new results in the Discussion. Although you might occasionally include in this section tables and figures which help explain something you are discussing, they must not contain new data (from your study) that should have been presented earlier. They might be flow diagrams, accumulation of data from the literature, or something that shows how one type of data leads to or correlates with another, etc. For example, if you were studying a membrane-bound transport channel and you discovered a new bit of information about its mechanism, you might present a diagram showing how your findings helps to explain the channel's mechanism.

WRITING A DISCUSSION [96]

The purpose of the Discussion is to state your interpretations and opinions, explain the implications of your findings, and make suggestions for future research. Its main function is to answer the questions posed in the Introduction, explain how the results support the answers and, how the answers fit in with existing knowledge on the topic. The Discussion is considered the heart of the paper and usually requires several writing attempts. The organization of the Discussion is important. Before beginning you should try to develop an outline to organize your thoughts in a logical form. You can use a cluster map, an issue tree, numbering, or some other organizational structure. The steps listed below are intended to help you organize your thoughts. If you need additional help see our articles *Eight Steps to Developing an Effective Manuscript Outline* and *Twelve Steps to Developing an Effective First Draft of your Manuscript* [96]. To make your message clear, the discussion should be kept as short as possible while clearly and fully stating, supporting, explaining, and defending your answers and discussing other important and directly relevant issues. Care must be taken to provide a commentary and not a reiteration of the results. Side issues should not be included, as these tend to obscure the message. No paper is perfect; the key is to help the reader determine what can be positively learned and what is more speculative. Interpret your data in the discussion *in appropriate depth*. This means that when you explain a phenomenon you must describe mechanisms that may account for the observation. If your results differ from your expectations, explain why that may have happened. If your results agree, then describe the theory that the evidence supported. It is never appropriate to simply state that the data agreed with expectations, and let it drop at that.

- Organize the Discussion from the specific to the general: your findings to the literature, to theory, to practice.
- Use the same key terms, the same verb tense (present tense), and the same point of view that you used when posing the questions in the Introduction.
- Begin by re-stating the hypothesis you were testing and answering the questions posed in the introduction.
- Support the answers with the results. Explain how your results relate to expectations and to the literature, clearly stating why they are acceptable and how they are consistent or fit in with previously published knowledge on the topic.
- Address all the results relating to the questions, regardless of whether or not the findings were statistically significant.
- Describe the patterns, principles, and relationships shown by each major finding/result and put them in perspective. The sequencing of providing this information is important; first state the answer, then the relevant results, then cite the work of others. If necessary, point the reader to a figure or table to enhance the "story".
- Defend your answers, if necessary, by explaining both why your answer is satisfactory and why others are not. Only by giving both sides to the argument can you make your explanation convincing.
- Discuss and evaluate conflicting explanations of the results. This is the sign of a good discussion.
- Discuss any unexpected findings. When discussing an unexpected finding, begin the paragraph with the finding and then describe it.
- Identify potential limitations and weaknesses and comment on the relative importance of these to your interpretation of the results and how they may affect the validity of the findings. When identifying limitations and weaknesses, avoid using an apologetic tone.
- Summarize concisely the principal implications of the findings, regardless of statistical significance.
- Provide recommendations (no more than two) for further research. Do not offer suggestions which could have been easily addressed within

the study, as this shows there has been inadequate examination and interpretation of the data.

- Explain how the results and conclusions of this study are important and how they influence our knowledge or understanding of the problem being examined.
- In your writing of the Discussion, discuss everything, but be concise, brief, and specific.
- Decide if each hypothesis is supported, rejected, or if you cannot make a decision with confidence. Do not simply dismiss a study or part of a study as "inconclusive".
- Research papers are not accepted if the work is incomplete. Draw what conclusions you can based upon the results that you have, and treat the study as a finished work.
- You may suggest future directions, such as how the experiment might be modified to accomplish another objective.
- Explain all of your observations as much as possible, *focusing on mechanisms*.
- Decide if the experimental design adequately addressed the hypothesis, and whether or not it was properly controlled.
- Try to offer alternative explanations if reasonable alternatives exist.

One experiment will not answer an overall question, so keeping the big picture in mind, where do you go next? The best studies open up new avenues of research. What questions remain? Recommendations for specific papers will provide additional suggestions. Researchers should be selecting the very important results obtained to interpret them in this section using the confirmation of the previous studies at the same line of research. Discussion section could be divided to sub-sections.

Style [96]

- When you refer to information, distinguish data generated by your own studies from published information or from information obtained from other students (verb tense is an important tool for accomplishing that purpose).
- Refer to work done by specific individuals (including yourself) in past tense.

- Refer to generally accepted facts and principles in present tense. For example, "Doofus, in a 1989 survey, *found* that anemia in basset hounds *was correlated* with advanced age. Anemia *is* a condition in which there *is* insufficient hemoglobin in the blood".

The biggest mistake that students make in discussions is to present a superficial interpretation that more or less re-states the results. It is necessary to suggest *why* results came out as they did, focusing on the mechanisms behind the observations.

Example of discussion section

4. Discussion

4.1. Chemical composition and condensed tannins

Lower levels of CP in browse during the DS *versus* the RS (Table 1) are consistent with other studies, which indicate that the minimum CP content of fodder tree leaves in the DS is more than twice that of grasses in the RS (Evitayani et al., 2004). Importantly, the CP content of browse species remained relatively high in *P. dulce* and *L. acapulcencis* during the DS, suggesting the possibility that leaves may be used as a DS fodder and feed supplement to low-quality diets. However, high secondary compound levels in *L. acapulcencis* may prevent its use if the nutrients cannot be digested and utilized. The higher

CP content in *P. dulce*, with its low CT during both seasons, suggests that it may be better quality forage for ruminants than the other browse species.

The CT content of browse species increased during the DS *versus* the RS, likely due to hydric stress in DS, activating enzymatic system phenylalanine ammonia-lyase (PAL) (Hidalgo, 2002) higher DS temperatures a finding consistent with those of Cabiddu et al. (2000) and Salem et al. (2006) for various browse species. Decreased concentrations of CT in browse leaves during the RS season may be due to the plant allocating more soluble carbohydrates to growth and reproduction than to producing tannins (Skogsmyr and Fagerstrom, 1992). This dilution effect during the RS may also explain the lower concentrations of fiber during the DS. Such seasonal variation in response to climatic and physiological changes in browse plants induces changes in chemical composition and, in particular, in concentrations of secondary compounds such as tannins (Salem, 2005; Salem et al., 2006). These differences determine the value of browse plant foliages as forages for ruminants.

4.2. Ruminal digestibility of browse species

Lower *in situ* degradability of browse species during the DS *versus* the humid RS in cows and goats could be due to the effects of CT on available N in leaves, which could reduce rumen ammonia concentrations and microbial growth (Salem et al., 2007). Cross-linkages of lignin to hemicellulose, polysaccharides and proteins may also depress digestibility (Van Soest, 1994). In the current study, the lignin content of RS browse was likely high, as suggested by the positive relationship between NDFom and ADFom in the studies of Frutos et al. (2002), and this could explain the lower of DM and NDF degradability of browse during the DS.

Differences between cows and goats in ruminal *in situ* degradability were probably due to differences in rumen microbial populations that affect the kinetics of rumen fermentation. In a comparison of sheep and goats, Salem et al. (2004) concluded that differences between sheep and goats in dentition, chewing/eating behaviour, gut physiology, compartment dimensions and retention time all influence gut microflora. Cone et al. (2002) compared rumen fluid from cows and sheep fed a similar diet, and reported that the volume of gas produced was lower with rumen fluid from sheep, although there was a good relationship between volumes of gas produced by the two sources of inocula. Bueno et al. (1999) compared bovine and ovine rumen fluid inocula adjusted to provide the same microbial mass and concluded that the two sources were comparable under tropical conditions.

Example (to be continued).

Animals that regularly consume tanniniferous feedstuffs adapt to minimize the detrimental effects of tannins. In our study, goats in AG, exposed for 3 months to diets containing 560 g/kg of a mixture of *P. dulce*, *Q. laeta* and *L. acapulcencis*, had higher nutrient *in situ* degradability than unadapted goats (UG) or cows. Wiryawan et al. (2000) observed that *in vitro* digestibility of *Caliandra* foliage was lowest in rumen fluid from goats fed grass, and increased when they were fed *Caliandra* for 3 months before the digestibility determinations. Similar results were reported by Tjakradidjaja et al. (2000) who observed that browse from high-tannin species (*Acacia* or *Caliandra*) were digested better by goats adapted to consuming high-tannin feedstuffs.

In goats, *in situ* degradability of browse species was higher in AG than in UG goats, which is consistent with McSweeney et al. (2001) who reported that within the same animal species responses to tanniniferous diets depend largely on the physiological capacity of the animals to adapt to the high-tannin diets. Mlambo et al. (2007) found that *in vitro* digestibility and fermentation kinetics of tannin-containing substrates improved when rumen fluid was obtained from goats fed a mixture of tannin-containing tree fruits (adapted rumen fluid). This is consistent with our finding that adapted goats had enhanced fermentative activity in the rumen to degrade high-tannin substrates, but this benefit was less evident with feedstuffs with lower concentrations of tannins.

Ruminants have a higher tolerance of tannins than non-ruminants (Smith et al., 2001), due to extra mastication, large amounts of saliva and rumen fermentation (Salem et al., 2001), and our results were likely due in part to acclimatization of microbial populations in the rumen. Odenyo and Osuji (1988) identified some tannin-tolerant ruminal bacterial strains from enriched cultures of rumen microflora of goats to establish a medium containing high concentrations of crude tannin extract or tannic acid. A strain of the anaerobe *Selenomonas ruminantium*, subspecies *ruminantium*, capable of growing on tannic acid or condensed tannin as a sole energy source, has been isolated from ruminal contents of feral goats browsing tannin-rich foliage (Skene and Brooker, 1995). Transferring these micro-organisms from feral goats to domestic goats and sheep fed tannin-rich foliage increased feed intake and N retention in inoculated *versus* uninoculated goats. Inoculation also improved N digestibility and reduced the rate of live weight loss in sheep and domestic goats (Miller et al., 1995).

Chapter 5

CONCLUSIONS, ACKNOWLEDGMENT AND REFERENCES

CONCLUSIONS

Conditions

- In this section it should be get a general statement reflex the objective from this study, and this will be the conclusion.
- Be careful to write a specific conclusion depending on the results obtained not a possibility case.
- It is not acceptable to add references in this section.
- Add the conclusion without any details of methodology or repetitions of the results section.

Examples

4. Conclusions

Degradability and fermentability of *A. saligna* leaves was affected by season for cattle and sheep, but not for buffalo, with reductions of in vitro gas production in the dry summer leaves. This may partly explain why animals avoid *A. saligna* leaves when foraging, especially late in the growing season. Buffalo rumen fluid inoculum had a higher ability to tolerate negative effects associated with increased concentrations of secondary components. While it may be possible to use sheep as models for cattle to characterize tanniniferous feeds (such as ASL), in vitro, it appears that neither cattle nor sheep rumen inoculum can be used as a model for buffaloes.

Example 1.

5. Conclusions

Higher nutritive value of browse species during the dry season for cows and goats could explain the great importance of those species in the nutrition of grazing ruminants in semi-arid regions of Mexico. *P. dulce* has potential to be used as protein source for sheep and goats during the dry season. Goats previously exposed to diets supplemented with the browse species were better able to degrade the browse species than goats fed diets not supplemented with browse species, which likely enables adapted goats to better use browse scrubland (Salem et al., 2006). Our results are consistent with the hypothesis that microbial populations in the rumen of goats fed a diet supplemented with the same browse species may evolve to become resistant to secondary compounds, in particularly condensed tannins, thereby becoming superior at degrading feedstuffs rich in condensed tannins.

Example 2.

5. Conclusions

The nutritional quality of the browse tree foliages *C. fistula*, *S. molle*, *C. speciosa* and *E. camaldulensis*, native to the semi-arid region of north Egypt, were evaluated by deter-mining levels of nutrients and secondary compounds, as well as feed intake and apparent digestibility in sheep and goats. Goats consumed 3.9% more DM than sheep per kg $BW^{0.75}$, and their digestibility was about 8% higher. Levels of CT (and due to its correlations, also TP, SAP, ALKA and EO) was a strong predictor of DM intake of PEG unsupplemented foliages in both sheep and goats. PEG increased intake of DM and its components in both sheep and goats, but levels of TP (and due to its correlations, also CT, SAP, ALKA and EO) was not a predictor of the proportional increase in DM with PEG feeding, which was best predicted by the level of CP within foliage (negative), which was improved by adding AF (positive) to the prediction. *C. speciosa*, had the highest nutrient value for both sheep and goats, both without and with PEG feeding, *S. molle* and *C. fistula* were intermediate and *E. camaldulensis* had the lowest nutritive value.

Example 3.

ACKNOWLEDGMENT

Conditions

In this section the authors will thanks any person or foundation had assistant in this work to be publish.

Examples

L.M. Camacho et al. / Animal Feed Science and Technology 155 (2010) 206–212 211

Acknowledgements

This work was undertaken with funds from the Universidad Autónoma del Estado de México (project UAEM 2400/2006U). Our gratitude also to the Mexican National Council for Science and Technology (Consejo Nacional de Ciencia y Tecnología-CONACYT) for the grant received by Luis Miguel Camacho Díaz.

Example 1.

Acknowledgements

The author thanks Dr. M.Z.M. Salem (Department of Timber Trees and Wood Technology) at the same university for his helpful in providing the collection of *A. saligna* leaves during the four seasons. Also, thanks to Dr. Y.M. Gohar (Division of Microbiology, Faculty of Science), for helpful comments and revision of the manuscript. I gratefully acknowledge

78   *A.-E.Z.M. Salem / Animal Feed Science and Technology 123–124 (2005) 67–79*

Dr. Caroline Rymer (Animal Science Research Group, University of Reading, UK) for assistance and advice during revision of the manuscript.

Example 2.

MANUSCRIPT LITERATURE CITED (REFERENCES)

Note: Although you should use these citation formats in this and other biology courses, specific formats vary considerably for individual journals. If you are trying to publish a paper in a specific journal, you will be required to follow the format of that journal. Some journals, e.g., *Science*, use a number system to give the text reference. That system will not be presented here, but you should expect to encounter it in your reading of the literature. A complete listing of citation formats for published materials may be found in Huth *et al.* [100].

Please note that in the introductory laboratory course, you will not be required to properly document sources of all of your information. One reason is that your major source of information is this website, and websites are inappropriate as primary sources. Second, it is problematic to provide a hundred students with equal access to potential reference materials. You may nevertheless find outside sources, and you should cite any articles that the instructor provides or that you find for yourself.

List all literature cited in your paper, in alphabetical order, by first author. In a proper research paper, only primary literature is used (original research articles authored by the original investigators). Be cautious about using web sites as references - anyone can put just about anything on a web site, and you have no sure way of knowing if it is truth or fiction. If you are citing an on line journal, use the journal citation (name, volume, year, page numbers). Some of your papers may not require references, and if that is the case simply state that "no references were consulted".

The Literature Cited section gives an alphabetical listing (by first author's last name) of the references that you actually cited in the body of your paper. Instructions for writing full citations [97] for various sources are given in on separate page. A complete format list for virtually all types of publication may be found in Huth *et al.* [100].

Note: Do not label this section "Bibliography". A bibliography contains references that you may have read but have not specifically cited in the text. Bibliography sections are found in books and other literary writing, but not scientific journal-style papers.

Citing References in the Body (Introduction and Discussion) of the Paper [100]

Throughout the body of your paper (primarily the Intro and Discussion), whenever you refer to outside sources of information, you must cite the sources from which you drew information. The simplest way to do this is to *parenthetically* give the author's last name and the year of publication, e.g., (Clarke, 2001). When citing information from another's publication, be sure to report the *relevant* aspects of the work clearly and succinctly, IN YOUR OWN WORDS. Provide a reference to the work as soon as possible after giving the information.

Standard Text Citation Formats [100]

There are exceptions among the various journals, but generally, in biological journals, the most frequent types of citations are shown in the following examples:

"It has been found that male mice react to estrogen treatment by a reduction in phase three of courtship behavior (Gumwad 1952:209; Bugjuice 1970). Click and Clack (1974) demonstrated that mice treated with synthetic estrogen analogs react similarly. The reduction in phase three courtship behavior may also be linked to nutritional status (Anon. 1996; Bruhahauser et al 1973)."

Note the following:

- Typically, *only the last name of the author(s) and the year of publication are given,e.g.,* Bugjuice 1970. Your Literature Cited section will contain the complete reference, and the reader can look it up there.
- Notice that the *reference to the book has a page number* (Gumwad 1952:209). This is to facilitate a reader's finding the reference in a long publication such as a book (not done for journal articles). The paper by Bugjuice (1970) is short, and if readers want to find the referenced information, they would not have as much trouble.
- For *two author papers*, give both authors' last names (e.g., Click and Clack 1974). Articles with more than two authors are cited by the first authors last name followed "and others" or "et al.", and then the year.
- When a book, paper, or article has *no identifiable author*, cite it as *Anon. Year, e.g.,* (Anon. 1996) (Anon. is the abbreviation for anonymous).
- If you want *reference a paper found in another article*, do so as follows: (Driblick 1923, *in* Oobleck 1978).
- A string of citations should be separated by semicolons, e.g., (Gumwad 1952:209; Bugjuice 1970; Bruhahauser et al 1973).
- Finally, you should note the *placement of the period* AFTER the parenthetical citation - the citation, too, is part of a sentence, e.g., "...courtship behavior (Gumwad 1952:209; Bugjuice 1970)".
- *Thesis:* Theses and dissertations should be cited as follows:
- Mortimer, R. 1975. A study of hormonal regulation of body temperature and consequences for reproductive success in the common house mouse (*Mus musculus*) in Nome, Alaska. Masters Thesis, University of Alaska, Anchorage. 83 p.
- *World Wide Web/Internet source citations [REVISED]:* WWW citation should be done with caution since so much is posted without peer review. When necessary, report the complete URL in the text

including the site author's name: "....(Gumwad, http://www.csu.edu /~gumwad/hormones/onlinepubs.html)"

- Internet sources should be included in your Literature Cited section.
- The Modern Language Association (MLA) has excellent guidelines for citing web-based sources in your Literature Cited list: http://www.mla.org/style_faq4.html
- For information on evaluating internet sources, look at: http://abacus .bates.edu/ils/web/research/evaluate.html
- For *unusual reference citations* such a government documents, technical reports, etc, refer to Huth et al (1994) for a complete listing of citation formats. A copy of this reference should be available in the Ladd Library and a copy is available in the Biology Department.

Personal Communications:

Suppose some of the information cited above was not gained from the Gumwad and Bugjuice publications, but rather in a personal conversation with or letter from an expert on the subject, Dr. Cynthia Mousse. When you have talked with, or written to someone, and gained some information or data that are not published, you should give credit to that person in the following way:

> "It has been found that male mice .... phase three of courtship behavior (C. Mousse, pers. comm.)."

- No date is entered for a personal communication, nor will it be entered in your Literature Cited section. However, the source is usually thanked in your Acknowledgments for their contribution.

Do Not the Following:

- *DO NOT USE FOOTNOTES*: Footnoting, although commonly done in books and other literary writing, is only *rarely* done in journal style papers. Cite references in the flow of the text as shown above.
- D*O NOT USE DIRECT QUOTES From Published Material:* In 99.99% of the cases, the information you want from a research article is an objective result or interpretation. How the author stated this information, i.e., *their prose*, is of little importance compared to the results or interpretations themselves. Take the information and *put it*

into your own words; avoid paraphrasing since this can potentially lead to plagiarism.

FORMATS FOR COMPLETE CITATIONS USED IN THE LITERATURE CITED [100]

In the Literature Cited you must provide complete citations for each of the published sources cited in your paper. The format for entries in the Literature Cited section differs for books and for journal papers because different kinds of information must be provided. The formats provided here are typical, but may vary in different publications depending on their particular needs and practices.

Some Basic Rules Applicable to All Formats Indexed by Author Name(S)

- *All citation entries* are listed in *alphabetical* order based the first author's *last* name
- If the same author(s) are cited for more than one paper *having the same order of authors' names*, the papers should be listed in *chronological sequence* by year of publication
- Authors' names MUST be listed in the citation in the same order as in the article
- If the same author(s) are cited for two or more papers published within the *same year,* place a small case letter after the year to denote the sequence in which you referred to them. For example:

Bugjuice, B. 1970a. Physiological effects of estrogen on mouse courtship behavior.....x.J Physiol 40(2):140-145.
Bugjuice, B. 1970b. Physiological effects of estrogen analogs: Insincere courtship xxxxbehavior in female mice. J Physiol 40(8):1240-1247.

- If no author is listed, use the word Anonymous in place of the author name(s)

Anonymous. 1992. .....give rest of citation using appropriate format

GENERAL CONDITIONS

Each journal had a guideline in writing the References in the manuscript, but generally we need to know how we can to write a Ref. of a research paper, meeting, thesis or book.

SPECIFIC FORMAT MODELS

Each model is shown as the full citation plus the in-text citation format.

Examples

Research paper reference:
Rule:

1.   Author/s name
2.   Year
3.   Paper Title
4.   Journal Name
5.   Volume
6.   Issue
7.   Pages number
   - Reference of One Author: Single author

Salem, A.Z.M. 2005. Impact of season of harvest on *in vitro* gas production and …. three ruminant species. *Anim. Feed Sci. Technol. 123-124, 67-79.*	Salem (2005) OR (Salem, 2005)

In the citation of Salem's paper, note the following:

- abbreviation of her first name; no comma (if full name is given, *then* use a comma); if multiple authors, use commas between;
- capitalization of the words in the title is just as though it were a sentence;

- abbreviation of the journal name; usually the header on the article will list the appropriate abbreviation for the journal; no periods in abbreviated form of journal name;
- "40" is the volume number "(2)" is the number of the issue; if no issue is given, the colon follows the volume number;
- "140-145" is the inclusive page numbers of the article;
- placement of periods is standard;
- indentation of the second line (and all subsequent lines) in the citation. This applies to all citations.

- *Reference of Two Authors:*

Titi, H., Lubbadeh W.F., 2004. Effect of feeding cellulase .... lactating ewes and goats. Small Rumin. Res. 52, 137–143.	Titi and Lubbadeh (2004)OR (Titi and Lubbadeh, 2004)

- *Reference of Three Authors:*

Varga, G.A., Dann, H.M., Ishler, V.A., 1998. The use of fiber concentrations..... J. Dairy Sci. 81, 3063–3074.	Varga, et al. (1998)OR (Varga, et al, 1998)

- *Reference of More than Three Authors: Multiple authors*

Ranilla, M.J. Tejido, M.L. Giraldo, L.A. Tricárico, J.M., Carro, M.D., 2008. Effects of an exogenous fibrolytic ......Anim. Feed. Sci. Technol. 145(1-4), 109-121.	Ranilla, et al. (2008)OR (Ranilla, et al, 2008)

- Author(s) Unknown or Not Named

If the authorship of a paper or other document is not provided, cite the author using the word "Anonymous" in the place of the author's name(s).

Anonymous. 1979. STD's and You: A Survival Guide for College Students ....in the 20th Century. Publ.#12-1979, Waazah County Health ....Department, Popville, Maine. 6 p.	Anonymous (1979) OR (Anonymous 1979)

Meeting or international conference reference
Rule:

1. Author name/s
2. Year
3. Paper Title
4. Conference Name
5. Location
6. Paper pages. (You can also mention if it is an abstract or full paper)

- References of One Author:

Makkar, H.P.S., 2000. Quantification of Tannins in Tree Foliage. A Laboratory Manual for the FAO/IAEA Coordinated Research Project on the Use of Nuclear and Related Techniques to Develop Simple Tannin Assays for Predicting and Improving the Safety and Efficiency of Feeding Ruminants on Tanniniferous Tree Foliage. FAO/IAEA Working Document, IAEA, Vienna, Austria, p. 38.	Makkar (2000) OR (Makkar, 2000)

- References of Two Authors:

Stokes, M.R., Zheng, S., 1995. The use of carbohydrase enzymes as feed additives for early lactation cows. 23rd Biennial Conf. Rumen Function, Chicago, IL, 23:35 (Abstract).	Stokes and Zheng (1995) OR (Stokes and Zheng, 1995)

- *References of More than two Authors:*

Salem, A.Z.M., González, J.S., López, S., Ranilla, M.J., 2000. The effect of feeding alfalfa treated with quebracho on parotid salivation in sheep. In: Van Arendonk, J.A.M. (Ed.), Proceedings of the 51st Annual Meeting of the European Association for Animal Production (EAAP), Session N5.17. Wageningen Press, The Hague, The Netherlands, p. 152.	Salem et al. (2000) OR (Salem et al., 2000)

Ph D and M Sc thesis reference
Rule:

1. Author name
2. Year of thesis
3. Thesis Title
4. Type of thesis
5. University Name

6. Location (city and country)

Example:

Salem, A.Z.M., 2002. Parotid saliva production and composition, feeding behavior, rumen fermentation, digestibility, and plasmatic parameters in sheep and goats: evolution of the response to the condensed tannins of quebracho in the diet. PhD Thesis. University of Leon, Leon, Spain.	Salem (2002) OR (Salem, 2002)

Book and Manual Reference
In the books citation, note the following:

- abbreviation of authors first name (one or both initials ok)
- capitalize title as if it was a sentence; the title is not underlined (contrary to literary format)
- "2nd ed." means second edition; if the book is a first edition; no entry is made, here, but if 2nd, 3rd, etc., then the notation is made
- give city of publication, and the name of the publisher
- year of publication follows authors' names
- placement of periods is standard
- indentation of all lines after the first

Rule:

1. Authors
2. Year>> Chapter Title
3. Book Title
4. Editors Name
5. Academic Published Book
6. Location>> Chapter Pages

Book: single author

Wong, E., 1973. Plant phenolics. In: Butler, G.W., Bailey, R.W. (Eds.), Chemistry and Biochemistry of Herbage. Academic Press, London, UK, pp. 265–322.	Wong (1973) OR (Wong 1973)

Book: multiple authors

Stewart, C.S., Flint, H.J., Byrant, M.P., 1997. The rumen bacteria. In: The rumen microbial ecosystem. 2nd ed. *Edited by* P.N. Hobson and C.S. Stewart. Blackie Academic and Professional, New York. pp. 10–55.	Stewart, *et al.* (1997) OR (Stewart, *et al.*, 1997)

Book: authors contributing a specific chapter

Kuret, J. and F. Murad. 1990. Adenohypophyseal hormones and related ....substances. In: Gilman A, Rall T, Nies A, Taylor P, editors. The ....pharmacological basis of therapeutics. 8th ed. New York: Pergamon. ....p. 1334-60.	Kuret and Murad (1990) OR (Kuret and Murad 1990)

Use the whole Book as reference

Steel, R.G.D., Torrie, J.H., 1980. Principles and Procedures of Statistics, 2nd ed. McGraw-Hill International, New York, NY, USA.	Steel and Torrie (1980) OR (Steel and Torrie, 1980)

ACKNOWLEDGEMENTS (INCLUDE AS NEEDED)

If, in your experiment, you received any significant help in thinking up, designing, or carrying out the work, or received materials from someone who did you a favor by supplying them, you must acknowledge their assistance and the service or material provided. Authors *always* acknowledge *outside reviewers* of their drafts (in PI courses, this would be done *only* if an instructor or other individual critiqued the draft prior to evaluation) and any *sources of funding* that supported the research. Although usual style requirements (e.g., 1st person, objectivity) are relaxed somewhat here, Acknowledgments are always brief and never flowery.

- Place the Acknowledgments between the Discussion and the Literature Cited.

APPENDICES

An Appendix contains information that is non-essential to understanding of the paper, but may present information that further clarifies a point without burdening the body of the presentation. An appendix is an *optional* part of the paper, and is only rarely found in published papers.

Each Appendix should be identified by a Roman numeral in sequence, e.g., Appendix I, Appendix II, etc. Each appendix should contain different material.

Some examples of material that might be put in an appendix (not an exhaustive list):

- raw data
- maps (foldout type especially)
- extra photographs
- explanation of formulas, either already known ones, or especially if you have "invented" some statistical or other mathematical procedures for data analysis
- specialized computer programs for a particular procedure
- full generic names of chemicals or compounds that you have referred to in somewhat abbreviated fashion or by some common name in the text of your paper
- diagrams of specialized apparati

Figures and Tables in Appendices

Figures and Tables are often found in an appendix. These should be formatted as discussed previously (see Tables and Figures), but are numbered in a separate sequence from those found in the body of the paper. So, the first Figure in the appendix would be Figure 1, the first Table would be Table 1, and so forth. In situations when multiple appendices are used, the Table and Figure numbering must indicate the appendix number as well.

REFERENCES

[1]   Thomson Reuters. Impact Factor Trend Graph [online]. 2008 [2010 June 12]. Available from: URL: http://scientific.thomsonreuters.com/tutorials/ jcr4/jcr4tut8.html

[2]   Thomson Reuters. Journal Summary List [online]. 2008 [2010 June 12]. Available from: URL: http://scientific.thomsonreuters.com/tutorials/ jcr4/jcr4tut5.html

[3]   Science Gateway. Journal Impact Factors [online]. 2010 [2010 May 12]. Available from: URL: http://www.sciencegateway.org/impact/

[4]   Gross, P. L. K. and Gross, E. M. (1927). College libraries and chemical education. *Science, 66, 385-389.*

[5]   Brodman, E. (1944). Methods of choosing physiology journals. *Bull. Med. Libr. Assn. 32, 479-483.*

[6]   Thomson Reuters. Journal Citation Reports [online]. 2010 [2010 June 12]. Available from: URL: http://thomsonreuters.com/products_services/ science/science_products/a-z/journal_citation_reports

[7]   Thomson Reuters. (1993). *SCI® Journal Citation Reports®: a bibliometric analysis of science journals in the ISI® database.* Philadelphia, PA: Institute for Scientific Information, Inc.®.

[8]   Thomson Reuters. Social Sciences Citation Index [online]. 2010 [2010 June 12]. Available from: URL: http://thomsonreuters.com/ products_services/science/science_products/a-z/social_sciences_citation_index

[9]   University of Washington Health Sciences Libraries. Impact Factors, *Journal Citation Reports (JCR)* [online]. 2009 [2009 October 18]. Available from: URL: http://healthlinks.washington.edu/howto/impactfactors.html#citation

[10] University of Washington Health Sciences Libraries. Impact Factors, *Eigenfactor* [online]. 2009 [2009 October 18]. Available from: URL: http://healthlinks.washington.edu/howto/impactfactors.html#eigen

[11] Garfield, E. (1970). Citation analysis as a tool in journal evaluation. *Science, 178, 471-479.*

[12] Garfield, E. (1970). Citation indexing for studying science. *Nature, 227, 669-671.*

[13] University of Washington Health Sciences Libraries. Impact Factors, *Journal Impact Factor* [online]. 2009 [2009 October 18]. Available from: URL: http://healthlinks.washington.edu/howto/impactfactors. html#jif

[14] University of Washington Health Sciences Libraries. Impact Factors, *Author Impact Factor* [online]. 2009 [2009 October 18]. Available from: URL: http://healthlinks.washington.edu/howto/impactfactors.html#aif

[15] Thomson Reuters. Journal Citation Reports Tutorial [online]. 2008 [2010 June 12]. Available from: URL: http://www.scientific.thomso n.com/tutorials/jcr4

[16] Cushing/ Whitney Medical Library, Yale University. Citation Analysis [online]. 2009 [2010 April 23]. Available from: URL: http://www.med. yale.edu/library/education/guides/citation

[17] Garfield, E. (1986). Which medical journals have the greatest impact? *Ann. Intern. Med., 105, 313-320.*

[18] The Thomson Corporation. Journal Citation Reports Help [online]. 2008 [2007 October 31]. Available from: URL: http://admin.isikn owledge.comJCR/help/h_fiveyr_if.htm#five_year_if

[19] The Thomson Corporation. Journal Citation Reports Help, *Journal* [online]. 2008 [2007 October 31]. Available from: URL: http://admin.isiknowledge.com/JCR/help/h_jrnlinfo.htm

[20] The Thomson Corporation. Journal Citation Reports Help, *Journal Title Changes* [online]. 2008 [2007 October 31]. Available from: URL: http://admin.isiknowledge.com/JCR/help/h_titlechanges.htm

[21] World Health Organization. WHO/ World Health Organization [online]. 2010 [2010 June 12]. Available from: URL: http://www.who.int/en/

[22] Ferrata Storti Foundation. Haematologica *the hematology journal*, Impact Factor [online]. 2010 [2010 June 12]. Available from: URL: http://online.haematologica.org/stats/if/

[23] EDP Sciences. 2007 Impact factor rises (June 2008) [online]. 2010 [2008 June 18]. Available from: URL: http://www.aanda.org/co ntent/view/315/43/lang,en/

[24] UOC Library. Journal impact factor [online]. 2010 [2010 January 08]. Available from: URL: http://biblioteca.uoc.edu/eng/index.html?services /factors

[25] Bergstrom, C. Why eigenfactor.org – ranking and mapping scientific journals [online]. 2009 [2010 July 26]. Available from: URL: http://eigenfactor.org/whyeigenfactor.htm

[26] Bergstrom, C. Why eigenfactor.org – ranking and mapping scientific journals [online]. 2009 [2010 July 26]. Available from: URL: http://www.eigenfactor.org/whyeigenfactor.htm

[27] Bergstrom, T., and McAfee, P. Journal cost-effectiveness 2009 BETA [online]. 2010 [2010 July 26]. Available from: URL: http://www. journalprices.com/

[28] Bergstrom, C. Cost-effectiveness search [online]. 2009 [2010 July 13]. Available from: URL: http://www.eigenfactor.org/pricesearch.php

[29] University of Washington health Sciences Libraries. Impact factors, H-Index [online]. 2010 [2009 October 18]. Available from: URL: http://healthlinks.washington.edu/howto/impactfactors.html#h

[30] University of Washington health Sciences Libraries. Impact factors, Cited References [online]. 2010 [2009 October 18]. Available from: URL: http://healthlinks.washington.edu/howto/impactfactors.html#cited

[31] University of Washington health Sciences Libraries. Impact factors, Web of Science (WoS) Cited references [online]. 2010 [2009 October 18]. Available from: URL: http://healthlinks.washington.edu/howto impactfactors.html#wos

[32] University of Washington health Sciences Libraries. Impact factors, Google Scholar (Beta) Cited References [online]. 2010 [2009 October 18]. Available from: URL: http://healthlinks.washington.edu/howto/ impactfactors.html#google

[33] University of Washington health Sciences Libraries. Impact factors [online]. 2010 [2009 October 18]. Available from: URL: http://health links.washington.edu/howto/impactfactors.html

[34] Hirsch, J. E. An index to quantify an individual's scientific research output [online]. 2005 [2005 September 29]. Available from: URL: http://arxiv.org/PS_cache/physics/pdf/0508/0508025v5.pdf

[35] Thomson Reuters. Web of Science Help [online]. 2009 [2009 February 17]. Available from: URL: http://images.isiknowledge.com/help/ WOS/hcr_citedau.html

[36] Matthews, T. Cited Reference Searching in the Web of Science [online]. 2007   [2009   February   24].   Available   from: URL: https://www.brainshark.com/brainshark/vu/view.asp?pi=34671484

[37] Cushing/ Whitney Medical Library. Citation Analysis, Cushing/Whitney Medical Library, Yale University [online]. 2009 [2010 July 13]. Available   from: URL: http://www.med.yale.edu/library/education/ guides/citation

[38] University of Washington health Sciences Libraries. Impact factors [online]. 2010 [2009 October 18]. Available from: URL: http://health links.washington.edu/howto/impactfactors.html

[39] Google. Google Scholar [online]. 2010 [2010 July 27]. Available from: URL: http://scholar.google.com/

[40] Thomson Reuters. Citation-Based and Descriptor-Based Search Strategies- Science- Thomson Reuters [online]. 2010 [2010 July 26]. Available   from: URL: http://thomsonreuters.com/products_services/ science/free/essays/citation_descriptor_strategies/

[41] Garfield, E. (1994). The concept of citation indexing: A unique and innovative tool for navigating the research literature. *Current Contents, 1-4,   3-5.*   Available   from: URL: http://thomsonreuters.com/ products_services/science/free/essays/concept_of_citation_indexing/

[42] Garfield, E. (1994). Where was this paper cited? *Current Contents, 5-8, 3-5.* Available from: URL: http://thomsonreuters.com/products_services/ science/free/essays/where_was_this_paper_cited/

[43] Spencer, C. C. (1967). Subject searching with Science Citation Index: Preparation of a drug bibliography using Chemical Abstracts, Index Medicus, and Science Citation Index 1961 and 1964. *American Documentation, 18(2), 87-96.*

[44] McCain, K. W. (1989). Descriptor and citation retrieval in the medical behavioral sciences literature: Retrieval overlaps and novelty distribution. *Journal of the American Society for Information Science, 40(2), 110-114.*

[45] Garfield, E. (1990). KeyWords Plus: ISI's breakthrough retrieval method. Part I. Expanding your searching power on Current Contents on Diskette. *Current Comments, 32, 295-299.*

[46] Journal Ranking. Journal Ranking [online]. 2006 [2010 July 17]. Available   from: URL: http://www.journal-ranking.com/ranking/ web/index.html

[47] Caprette, D. R./ Rice University. How to write a research paper [online].
      1995 [2007 August 20]. Available from: URL: http://www.ruf.rice.edu/~
      bioslabs/tools/report/reportform.html

[48] Bates College, Department of Biology. *How to write a paper in
      scientific journal style and format* [online]. 2002 [2008 September 25].
      Available   from: URL: http://abacus.bates.edu/~ganderso/biology/
      resources/writing/HTWsections.html

[49] Kupsh, J. Writing examples [online]. 1995 [2007 August 20]. Available
      from: URL:
      http://www.ruf.rice.edu/~bioslabs/bios211/rice_only/Writing_examples.
      pdf

[50] Alves, B. Hum 1 – *Writing an introduction* [online]. 2010 [2009 June
      29]. Available from: URL: http://www2.hmc.edu/~alves/intros.html

[51] Alves, B. Hum 1 – *The thesis statement* [online]. 2010 [2009 June 29].
      Available from: URL: http://www2.hmc.edu/~alves/thesis.html

[52] The Writing Center, University of North Carolina at Chapel Hill.
      Introductions [online]. 2007 [2010 July 25]. Available from: URL:
      http://www.unc.edu/depts/wcweb/handouts/introductions.html

[53] The Writing Center, University of North Carolina at Chapel Hill.
      Conclusions [online]. 2007 [2010 July 25]. Available from: URL:
      http://www.unc.edu/depts/wcweb/handouts/conclusions.html

[54] Rose, L./ John Wiley and Sons, Inc. *Journal of the History of the
      Behavioral Sciences* . Author Guidelines [online]. 2010 [2010 July 26].
      http://www3.interscience.wiley.com/journal/31970/home/ForAuthors.ht
      ml

[55] Bates College, Department of Biology. *How to write guide: Sections of
      the paper* [online]. 2008 [2008 September 25]. Available from: URL:
      http://abacus.bates.edu/~ganderso/biology/resources/writing/HTWsectio
      ns.html

[56] Bates College, Department of Biology. *How to write guide: Sections of
      the paper* [online]. 2008 [2008 September 25]. Available from: URL:
      http://abacus.bates.edu/~ganderso/biology/resources/writing/HTWscctio
      ns.html#introliterature

[57] Bates College, Department of Biology. *How to write guide: How to cite
      other papers in your paper* [online]. 2008 [2008 September 10].
      Available   from: URL: http://abacus.bates.edu/~ganderso/biology/
      resources/writing/HTWcitations.html

[58] Bates College, Department of Biology. *How to write guide: Sections of
      the paper, Introduction* [online]. 2008 [2008 September 25]. Available

from: URL: http://abacus.bates.edu/~ganderso/biology/resources/
writing/HTWsections.html#intropurpose

[59] Bates College, Department of Biology. *How to write guide: Sections of
the paper, Introduction* [online]. 2008 [2008 September 25]. Available
from: URL: http://abacus.bates.edu/~ganderso/biology/resources/
writing/HTWsections.html#introrationale

[60] Caprette, D. R./ Rice University. *How to write a research paper*
[online]. 1995 [2007 August 20]. Available from: URL: http://www.ru
f.rice.edu/~bioslabs/tools/report/reportform.html

[61] Bates College, Department of Biology. *How to write guide: Sections of
the paper* [online]. 2008 [2008 September 25]. Available from: URL:
http://abacus.bates.edu/~ganderso/biology/resources/writing/HTWsectio
ns.html

[62] Bates College, Department of Biology. *How to write guide: Sections of
the paper, Title, authors' names, and institutional affiliations* [online].
2008   [2008   September   25].   Available   from: URL:
http://abacus.bates.edu/~ganderso/biology/resources/writing/HTWsectio
ns.html#title

[63] Bates College, Department of Biology. *How to write guide: How to cite
other sources in your paper* [online]. 2008 [2008 September 10].
Available   from: URL: http://abacus.bates.edu/~ganderso/biology
/resources/writing/HTWcitations.html

[64] Bates College, Department of Biology. *How to write guide: Sections of
the paper, Discussion* [online]. 2008 [2008 September 25]. Available
from: URL: http://abacus.bates.edu/~ganderso/biology/resources/
writing/HTWsections.html#discussion

[65] Bates College, Department of Biology. *How to write guide: Sections of
the paper, Materials and methods* [online]. 2008 [2008 September 25].
Available   from: URL: http://abacus.bates.edu/~ganderso/biology/
resources/writing/HTWsections.html#methods

[66] Bates College, Department of Biology. *How to write guide: How to cite
other papers in your paper, Citing references in the body (intro and
discussion) of the paper* [online]. 2008 [2008 September 10]. Available
from: URL: http://abacus.bates.edu/~ganderso/biology/resources/
writing/HTWcitations.html#text

[67] The Writing Center, University of North Carolina at Chapel Hill.
Reading assignments [online]. 2007 [2010 July 25]. Available from:
URL: http://www.unc.edu/depts/wcweb/handouts/readassign.html

[68] Rose, L./ John Wiley and Sons, Inc. *Journal of the History of the Behavioral Sciences* . Author Guidelines [online]. 2010 [2010 July 26]. http://www3.interscience.wiley.com/journal/31970/home/ForAuthors.ht ml?CRETRY=1andSRETRY=0

[69] Bates College, Department of Biology. *How to write guide: Sections of the paper, Materials and methods, Describe the organism(s) used in the study* [online]. 2008 [2008 September 25]. Available from: URL: http://abacus.bates.edu/~ganderso/biology/resources/writing/HTWsectio ns.html#subjects

[70] Bates College, Department of Biology. *How to write guide: Sections of the paper, Materials and methods, Describe the site where your field study was conducted* [online]. 2008 [2008 September 25]. Available from: URL: http://abacus.bates.edu/~ganderso/biology/resources/ writing/HTWsections.html#describesite

[71] Bates College, Department of Biology. *How to write guide: Sections of the paper, Materials and methods, Describe your experimental design clearly* [online]. 2008 [2008 September 25]. Available from: URL: http://abacus.bates.edu/~ganderso/biology/resources/writing/HTWsectio ns.html#experimentaldesign

[72] Bates College, Department of Biology. *How to write guide: Sections of the paper, Materials and methods, Describe the protocol for your study in sufficient detail that other scientists could repeat your work to verify your findings* [online]. 2008 [2008 September 25]. Available from: URL: http://abacus.bates.edu/~ganderso/biology/resources/writing/HTW sections.html#protocol

[73] Bates College, Department of Biology. *How to write guide: Sections of the paper, Materials and methods, Describe how the data were summarized and analyzed* [online]. 2008 [2008 September 25]. Available from: URL: http://abacus.bates.edu/~ganderso/biology /resources/writing/HTWsections.html#dataanalysis

[74] Bates College, Department of Biology. *How to write guide: Sections of the paper, Materials and methods, Describe the protocol for your study in sufficient detail that other scientists could repeat your work to verify your findings* [online]. 2008 [2008 September 25]. Available from: URL: http://abacus.bates.edu/~ganderso/biology/resources/writing/ HTWsections.html#protocol

[75] Bates College, Department of Biology. *How to write guide: Sections of the paper, Materials and methods, Describe how the data were summarized and analyzed* [online]. 2008 [2008 September 25].

Available   from: URL: http://abacus.bates.edu/~ganderso/biology/
resources/writing/HTWsections.html#dataanalysis

[76] Bates College, Department of Biology. *How to write guide: Sections of
the paper, Section headings* [online]. 2008 [2008 September 25].
Available   from: URL: http://abacus.bates.edu/~ganderso/biology/
resources/writing/HTWsections.html#headings

[77] Bates College, Department of Biology. *Resource materials:
Experimental design worksheet* [online]. 2008 [2005 October 29].
Available   from: URL: http://abacus.bates.edu/~ganderso/biology/
resources/cxpdesign.html

[78] Bates College, Department of Biology. *IIow to write guide: How to cite
other papers in your paper, Citing references in the body (intro and
discussion) of the paper* [online]. 2008 [2008 September 10]. Available
from: URL: http://abacus.bates.edu/~ganderso/biology/resources/writing
/HTWcitations.html#text

[79] Caprette, D. R./ Rice University. Common errors in student research
papers [online]. 1996 [2007 August 20]. Available from: URL:
http://www.ruf.rice.edu/~bioslabs/tools/report/reporterror.html

[80] Caprette, D. R./ Rice University. Writing rules [online]. 2002 [2007
August 20]. Available from: URL: http://www.ruf.rice.edu/~bioslabs/
tools/report/wrules.html

[81] Beason, B./ Rice University. Writing the scientific article [online]. 1999
[2005   December   21].   Available   from: URL:
http://www.owlnet.rice.edu/~bios311/bios311/sciarticle.html

[82] American Society for Biochemistry and Molecular Biology. *The Journal
of Biological Chemistry*: Editorial Policies, Practices and Guidelines
[online]. 2010 [2010 March 22]. Available from: URL: http://www.j
bc.org/site/misc/edpolicy.xhtml

[83] American Society of Animal Science. *Journal of Animal Science
Instructions for Authors* [online]. 2010 [2010 July 27]. Available from:
URL: http://jas.fass.org/misc/JAS_Instruct_to_Authors_10.pdf

[84] Bates College, Department of Biology. *How to write guide: A strategy
for writing up research results* [online]. 2008 [2008 September 25].
Available   from: URL: http://abacus.bates.edu/~ganderso/biology/
resources/writing/HTWstrategy.html#abstract

[85] Koopman, P./ Carnegie Mellon University. How to write an abstract
[online]. 1997 [2010 July 27]. Available from: URL: http://www.ece.c
mu.edu/~koopman/essays/abstract.html

[86] Undergraduate Research Berkeley. *How to write an abstract: Links and tips* [online]. 2010 [2003 October 14]. Available from· URL: http://research.berkeley.edu/ucday/abstract.html

[87] Bates College, Department of Biology. *How to write a paper in scientific journal style and format* [online]. 2008 [2008 September 25]. Available from: URL: http://abacus.bates.edu/~ganderso/biology/resources/writing/HTWstrategy.html

[88] Writing Development Centre, Newcastle University. Results [online]. 2010 [2009 July 20]. Available from: URL: http://www.ncl.ac.uk/students/wdc/learning/theses/structure/results.htm

[89] Caprette, D. R./ Rice University. How to write a research paper [online]. 1995 [2007 August 20]. Available from: URL: http://www.ruf.rice.edu/~bioslabs/tools/report/reportform.html

[90] Bates College, Department of Biology. How to write guide: Sections of the paper [online]. 2008 [2008 September 25]. Available from: URL: http://abacus.bates.edu/~ganderso/biology/resources/writing/HTWsections.html

[91] Bates College, Department of Biology. How to write guide: A strategy for writing up research results [online]. 2008 [2008 September 25]. Available from: URL: http://abacus.bates.edu/~ganderso/biology/resources/writing/HTWstrategy.html#results

[92] Bates College, Department of Biology. How to write guide: A strategy for writing up research results, Results [online]. 2008 [2008 September 25]. Available from: URL: http://abacus.bates.edu/~ganderso/biology/resources/writing/HTWstrategy.html

[93] Bates College, Department of Biology. How to write guide: A strategy for writing up research results, Making tables and figures [online]. 2008 [2008 September 25]. Available from: URL: http://abacus.bates.edu/~ganderso/biology/resources/writing/HTWtablefigs.html

[94] Gerwien, R./ Bates College, Department of biology. Painless guide to statistics [online]. 2008 [2008 September 26]. Available from: URL: http://abacus.bates.edu/~ganderso/biology/resources/statistics.html

[95] Lawson, TG; Gronros, DL; Evans, PE; Bastien, MC; Michalewich, KM; Clark, JK; Edmonds, JH; Graber, KH; Werner, JA; Lurvey, BA; Cate,JM. (1999). Identificaction and characterization of a protein destruction signal in the Encephalomyocarditis virus 3c protease. *The Journal of Biological Chemistry, 274, 9871-9980.*

[96] San Francisco Edit. San Francisco Edit [online]. 2008 [2010 July 26]. Available from: URL: http://www.sfedit.net/newsletters.htm

[97] Bates College, Department of Biology. How to write guide: How to cite other sources in your paper [online]. 2008 [2008 September 10]. Available from: URL: http://www.bates.edu/~ganderso/biology/resources/writing/HTWcitations.html

[98] Bates College, Department of Biology. How to write guide: How to cite other papers in your paper, Citing references in the body (intro and discussion) of the paper [online]. 2008 [2008 September 10]. Available from: URL: http://abacus.bates.edu/~ganderso/biology/resources/writing/HTWcitations.html#text

[99] Bates College, Department of Biology. How to write guide: How to cite other papers in your paper, Citing references in the body (intro and discussion) of the paper [online]. 2008 [2008 September 10]. Available from: URL: http://abacus.bates.edu/~ganderso/biology/resources/writing/HTWcitations.html#text

[100] Huth, J; Brogan, M; Dancik, B; Kommedahl, T; Nadziejka, D; Robinson, P; Swanson, W. (1994). *Scientific format and style: The CBE manual for authors, editors, and publishers.* Cambridge: Cambridge University Press.

[101] K. Tajima and T.Nagamine, http://mx.images.search.yahoo.com/images/view?back=http%3A%2F%2Fmx.images.search.yahoo.com%2Fsearch%2Fimages%3Fp%3Drumen%2Bmicroorganisms%26ei%3DUTF8%26fr%3Dyfp706&w=367&h=408&imgurl=dgc.ac.affrc.go.jp%2FDGCtpc%2Fnagamine%2F4.rumenfungi.JPG&rurl=http%3A%2F%2Fdgc.ac.affrc.go.jp%2FDGCtpc%2Fnagamine%2Ftopic4.html&size=27k&name=4+rumenfungi+JPG&p=rumen+microorganisms&oid=a40f469037133d5e&fr2=&no=7&tt=27&sigr=11lo83ldh&sigi=11j2vtrdg&sigb=12s9nd03h&type=JPG

INDEX